Enhancing Practice through Classroom Research

A teacher's guide to professional development

Caitriona McDonagh, Mary Roche, Bernie Sullivan and Máirín Glenn

Routledge
Taylor & Francis Group

LONDON AND NEW YORK

First published 2012
by Routledge
2 Park Square, Milton Park, Abingdon, Oxon OX14 4RN

Simultaneously published in the USA and Canada
by Routledge
711 Third Avenue, New York, NY 10017

Routledge is an imprint of the Taylor & Francis Group, an informa business

British Library Cataloguing in Publication Data
A catalogue record for this book is available from the British Library

Library of Congress Cataloging in Publication Data
Enhancing practice through classroom research : a teacher's guide to
professional development / Caitriona McDonagh . . . [et al.].
    p. cm.
    Includes bibliographical references and index.
    1. Teachers—In-service training. 2. Teachers—Professional relationships.
    3. Reflective teaching. I. McDonagh, Caitriona.
    LB1731.E542 2012
    371.1—dc23
    2011025972

ISBN: 978–0–415–59767–8 (hbk)
ISBN: 978–0–415–59768–5 (pbk)
ISBN: 978–0–203–14620–0 (ebk)

Typeset in Times New Roman & Gill Sans
by Swales & Willis Ltd, Exeter, Devon

MIX
Paper from
responsible sources
FSC® C004839
www.fsc.org

Printed and bound in Great Britain by
TJ International Ltd, Padstow, Cornwall

Contents

Acknowledgements

We are grateful to everyone who helped us write this book. We would like to thank especially our husbands and families, who supported us throughout. We are also very thankful to our school communities, colleagues and the children in our classrooms who inspired us to see the world anew.

Introduction

This book aims to contribute to your empowerment as a teacher by indicating to you that you have the potential to become influential in your own educational settings (Carr and Kemmis 1986; Schön 1995; Whitehead and McNiff 2006). It encourages you to become a more autonomous professional as you undertake educational research. We hope this book will inspire you to engage in enquiry, to develop a critical and questioning disposition, and to have the confidence to theorise your practice as you study for formal accreditation.

There is a growing trend in educational contexts for teachers to develop, not just as competent and capable practitioners, but also as generators of educational theory, and we plan to help you to begin such a process for yourself. When we refer to 'we', we are speaking about ourselves, the authors of the book, and we are hopeful that you, our reader, will find that our book guides you not only as you try to make sense of the challenges that you experience in your workplace, but also as you engage in formal studies at postgraduate level.

We authors came together in the late 1990s through an action research study group established in Ireland by Jean McNiff. We all subsequently studied for our PhDs in the University of Limerick and became part of a collaborative study group along with Jean and other doctoral students. While our research interests and contexts varied widely, we all embraced a form of self-study action research that is based on the idea of generating theory from our work practice. Most of our research, at both Master's and PhD level, was undertaken with the supervision and support of a tutor. We reflected deeply on our work and collaborated in exploring one another's ideas in a highly critical, but respectful, manner. We read widely and voraciously and shared our most current ideas. We gathered data and established criteria by which we could present it as evidence of our claim to knowledge. We concluded our studies and, as well as continuing our friendship, we formed a close professional collaboration. Our passion for self-study action research, and our hope that more policy makers and academics would explore its possibilities as a life-enhancing form of research, motivated the writing of this book.

The book is structured in the form of an action research process with vignettes from our own research accounts. It is geared towards busy educators and will focus on guiding you through the process of tailoring your professional development and research to suit your individual educational needs and contexts. We take you through the research process as we experienced it. Based on our research experiences, we show how you can use your accounts to generate new personal theories of practice for yourself, through taking a classroom action research approach to professional development. For you, this will involve identifying your educational concerns, as Whitehead and McNiff (2006) suggest, and looking at an aspect of your work that is of interest to you; asking why you might be concerned; taking actions as you endeavour to improve your practice; and developing your educational theory as you come to realise the significance of your work. Through this book we aim to guide you through a similar process of reflection and action as you seek to improve your practice or your understanding of it.

The idea of taking action to improve the work setting can be traced back to Kurt Lewin, a social psychologist and educationalist, who coined the phrase 'action research' in the 1940s. Stephen Corey, who brought action research to the fore in education in the USA in the 1950s, believed that by studying their teaching, teachers are more likely to improve their practice. Since the 1970s the idea of taking action and researching simultaneously has taken on new directions and new names. John Elliott, in the UK, talks about an interpretive action research approach where the researcher investigates the practices of others. Wilf Carr and Stephen Kemmis focus on the teacher as a researcher with self-reflective action enquiry. Jack Whitehead and Jean McNiff developed a living theory approach to action research where practitioners ask 'How do I improve what I am doing?' Over time the shifting focus of action research has given rise to various approaches to classroom research with many features in common.

In this book we use a self-study action research approach as we explain our classroom research, which aims towards enhanced understanding of practice, transformation of practice and the generation of theory. McNiff and Whitehead suggest that in traditional social science research the researcher 'stands outside the research situation and observes what other people are doing', which means that researchers 'adopt an outsider or spectator perspective' (2010: 11). However, in our classroom research we focus on our own work and our own learning, along with others, so we adopt an insider, participant perspective and thus the researcher becomes 'the centre of the research' (2010: 11). We invite you to adopt a similar stance.

Noffke and Somekh talk about how there has been a worldwide growth in interest in action research in the past 20 years. It is a methodology that is suited to

> exploring, developing and sustaining change processes both in classrooms and whole organizations. . . . Action research has become a prominent methodology taught to doctoral and masters level . . . in many major institutions. . . . It is widely accepted as a means of supporting school-based professional development . . . and as part of a certification schemes in many countries.
>
> (Noffke and Somekh 2009: 1)

It is clear that Noffke and Somekh view an action research methodology as appropriate for personal and professional development programmes and for accreditation in the university.

Our book is useful for educators who want to explore some ideas around researching their own practice for the purpose of academic accreditation. One of the key features of action research is its 'participatory, "grass-roots" quality' (Noffke and Somekh 2009: 1) and so the personal story of the researcher, their reflections and their ability to engage in critical thinking are very important. We are embracing a self-study action research approach to educational research that involves aspects of participatory action research, critical action research, class-room research, self-study, narrative inquiry, critical pedagogy, action learning, reflective practice and so on. Like Noffke and Somekh (2009), we want to avoid 'simplistic divisions between different kinds of action research which always tend to produce a hierarchy of status/worth' (2009: 1), a battle of hierarchy that is not helpful to our research process.

LaBoskey (2004) considers the following four aspects of self-study to be integral to the research process:

1   aiming towards improvement in practice and/or thinking
2   collaboration and communication with colleagues and students, and critical engagement with the literature
3   the utilisation of multiple methods of data collation to gain in-depth under-standing
4   sharing the research with the education community.

We embrace LaBoskey's ideas in this book as well as the idea that while we are undertaking research on ourselves and our work, we are also working along with others and seeking to improve their experience in education. We also embed Cochran-Smith's idea of 'inquiry as stance' (2009) in our approach to classroom research. We adopt Whitehead and McNiff's (2006) ideas around putting 'I' at the centre of the research. We seek to develop a theory from practice, and in that process we show with evidence collated in various data collection strategies how we can offer descriptions and explanations that support the validity of our theory. We make our work public and share our findings with other interested parties as we seek to influence colleagues and perhaps influence policy.

We describe and explain how we identified our educational values, worked towards a realisation of these values in our day-to-day classroom practice, and generated theory in the process. The concept of educational values is a recur-rent theme throughout this book. It is widely acknowledged that action research, especially a self-study approach, is a value-laden form of enquiry (Bassey 1990; Bullough and Pinnegar 2004; Elliott 1991; McNiff and Whitehead 2010; Somekh and Zeichner 2009). Our research approach involves the identification, naming and scrutiny of our personal educational values: 'Throughout ask yourself if your action research project is helping you (and those with whom you work) and the extent to which you are *living your educational values*' (italics in original) (Cohen, Manion and Morrison 2007: 309).

Our values are the all-encompassing framework of how we are and how we work in our classrooms. They are the guiding principles of our research and act as the criteria by which we evaluate the validity of our work and the standards against which we test our claims to knowledge (Whitehead and McNiff 2006). The concept of values, therefore, will be a feature of every chapter.

A word to the reader

Our book includes eight main chapters and a concluding chapter. Each chapter constitutes a stage of a self-study action research project and builds on the previous one, so that by the end of the book you will have created a simple draft of your research account, or you will have experienced a cycle of a self-study action research project. Its structure is based on our own and McNiff and Whitehead's (2011) interpretation of an action research approach. We have used the following 'I' questions because of our focus on personal professional development:

- How do I identify a research question?
- How do I link values in my practice and values in research?
- How do I reflect on and develop a better understanding of practice?
- How can I think critically about my work?
- How do I take practical steps to advance my research topic?
- How do I establish the relevance of major research paradigms to my work?
- How do I analyse data and use professional values as standards of judgement?
- How do I develop theory from practice, disseminate it and understand its significance?

To help you to engage personally with this book, each chapter is designed to promote reflection through questions and/or specific tasks.

Chapter 1 explores how we identify an area for research. This could be a subject that causes the teacher–researcher disquiet. Mary Roche introduces you to the concept of educational values and shows how they act as guiding principles for your practice. She shows how she made many errors and continued to teach didactically despite knowing that she valued the idea of pupil voice and discussion. You are provided with a series of reflective questions to help you articulate some core values. You are encouraged to read professional literature and identify texts that you find 'transformative'.

Chapter 2 explores how values act as conceptual frameworks for the research process. Mary Roche continues by showing how she began transforming her practice as she recognised that care, freedom and justice were core concepts for her research. Taking one concept, care, as an example, she provides case studies from her classroom to show how she began to research and theorise her practice. As she reflected on the concept of care she began to learn to be more critically aware in the process. You, the reader, are guided through the beginning this process for yourself. The importance of reading for professional development is stressed throughout.

Chapter 3 encourages the researcher to ask questions like 'Why am I concerned?' Máirín Glenn outlines how self-study action research is frequently not a linear process and that it often can become complex. The role of reflective practice in practitioner research in the classroom is discussed along with an outline of how a reflective journal can enhance the reflective process. It emphasises the importance of critical thinking. The ideas of 'praxis' is discussed along with the importance of focusing the research on oneself along with others. The developing of a new sense of awareness of what is happening in one's everyday work is also explored. You are reminded of the importance of engaging with literature so as to enhance the research.

Máirín Glenn continues to explore ideas around why one might be interested in particular aspects of one's work in Chapter 4. Whitehead's thinking (1989) around 'experiencing oneself as a living contradiction' is explored and explained; this thinking can be a cornerstone of an action research process. Some ideas of critical pedagogy are examined and located in the everyday practices of the educator. The latter part of the chapter provides a model that you could use to examine the reasons why you might focus on specific aspects of your practice.

In Chapter 5 Caitriona McDonagh puts forward a five step practical plan to advance your chosen research topic. It offers suggestions on how to gather accurate and relevant information as your situation progresses. There are explanations of the importance of grounding your information gathering methods in your personal ontological and epistemological values. The requirements for engaging in ethical research *with* participants rather than *on* participants are teased out. Thus the data-gathering methods described can be participatory, value informed and suitable for fluid research situations. These are all key features of classroom action research, which aims to support professional development.

Chapter 6 shows how to question the practical relevance of three research paradigms – empirical, interpretive and action research – common in social and educational research. Caitriona McDonagh considers their practical relevance to readers' particular research issues at three levels:

1   their relevance to the teaching profession by examining the world view that underpins each paradigm
2   how each paradigm can support teacher autonomy and personal professional development as part of the research process
3   how the writing of your research report can potentially contribute to the knowledge base of the teaching profession.

Chapter 7 focuses on the process of data analysis as one reaches the end of the research project and attempts to make sense of it. Bernie Sullivan indicates the need for critical analysis in the search for improvement in practice, in understanding one's practice or in one's thinking processes. She also discusses the importance of providing corroborative evidence through triangulation from other sources, in order to strengthen the validity of one's findings. The reader is introduced to the idea of using one's values as the standards of judgement for assessing the research findings, and examining whether one is living out these values in one's practice (Whitehead and McNiff 2006).

In Chapter 8 Bernie Sullivan introduces the reader to the idea of developing a theory of practice through reflecting on the research findings. This process occurs as the researcher articulates the new knowledge emerging from the research. The new knowledge can be considered a theory of practice, having evolved from the researcher's continuous critical reflection on practice. This chapter also engages with the idea of dissemination of research findings so that others may benefit from the new knowledge and perhaps be encouraged to engage in similar research projects. The educational influence resulting from this dissemination would increase the significance of the research.

Professional development and educational research

> Research is about generating knowledge. Action research creates knowledge based on enquiries conducted within specific and often practical contexts . . . the purpose of action research is to learn through action leading to personal or professional development.
>
> (Koshy 2009: 4)

When we each began on our personal journeys of enquiry into our teaching lives we were seeking personal and professional development such as suggested by Koshy (2009) above. Gradually, we refined our search for a suitable methodology into a self-study action research approach. As a methodological tool, self-study is aimed at improving practice and can be 'the focal point for studying the intersection between theory and practice' (Russell 2002: 9, cited in Scherff and Kaplan 2006: 155). Bullock argues that 'self-study as a basis for knowing about and inquiring into teacher education practices is a well-established research methodology'. He goes on:

> Zeichner (2007, p. 40) recently criticized the self-study community for focusing on the 'methodological aspects of the research rather than on the content of what has been learned from the research and how it builds on what others have learned,' and challenged the community to develop ways to share some of the substantive knowledge of what has been learned since the genesis of self-study methodology in the 1990s.
>
> (Bullock 2009: 293)

We would like to think that we are meeting Zeichner's challenge as we share the content of what we have learned throughout the chapters of this book.

Reviewing self-study action research as a means of carrying out educational enquiry, Bass, Anderson-Patten and Allender state that self-study offers 'research that puts us in touch with who we are, what we do, and how we change . . . [so] we can grow as we continuously learn to teach' (2002: 68). They also suggest that 'self study is an emergent and creative process, that change in practice necessarily integrates change in self, that self-study requires a collective and that self-study's version of professional growth challenges the developmental model that implies that teachers improve simply with experience' (2002: 5).

Our research examples in this book show the dynamic process involved that did indeed necessitate a change, not only in how we worked, but also in how we thought and began to view the world of education. We can attest also to the need for a 'collective': we believe that we could not have gained as much understanding about our different educational contexts and pedagogical approaches without the support of our supervisor and critical friends.

Our research set out to generate new knowledge, initially for ourselves, in order to deepen our understanding of why we teach as we do, but also, through disseminating our research, we took up Zeichner's (2007) challenge as outlined earlier so as to encourage others like you to develop as autonomous professionals. Our research was cited by McNiff and Whitehead (2005) as they explained the idea of 'teacher as researcher' (Stenhouse 1975) and 'teacher as educational theorist'. We promote both stances as we suggest ways in which you may enhance your practice through classroom research and develop professionally. We do this at two levels:

1   by demonstrating the logical and methodological meanings in our pedagogical practices
2   by explaining how we judge our professional practices by our identified critical living criteria, which are grounded in our ontological and epistemological values.

We invite you to use our examples as a springboard for reconceptualising yourself as a reflective professional while you tailor your own process of personal and professional growth and work towards postgraduate accreditation. Like Bullock, we do not wish to offer you 'a prescriptive set of propositions . . . but a set of personal understandings constructed partly through reading research on education and partly through engaging in self-study of [your] developing pedagogy' (2009: 302).

Traditionally classroom research has been drawn from a social science model that is grounded in social control. We encourage moving from this model to one grounded instead in 'participative social evolution' (McNiff 2002: 3). Elliott suggests that professional development should be about 'trusting teachers in their capacities to exercise wisdom and judgement' (2004a: 170, cited in McNamara and O'Hara 2008: 8). We feel that we have begun this process for ourselves and we offer our accounts as evidence.

We hope that this book goes beyond introducing you to the idea of self-study action research or encouraging you to engage in postgraduate study. We want you to experience our enjoyment in this form of research.

Part I

Thinking professionally and reflecting on practice

Mary Roche

If you are a classroom teacher, reading this book could be seen as evidence that you are interested in professional improvement and that you hold a value of care about your work. I could also make an assumption that you care because you know that what you do daily may have profound influence on, and significance for, the lives of others, particularly those of your pupils. It is likely that you are the kind of teacher who is always on the look-out for anything that will help you to be a better teacher – because of this highly developed sense of care and professionalism. Perhaps you care about your professional development enough to engage in studies for a Master's degree so as to advance further in your career in education. You may now wish to research an area of your practice and are looking for some ideas about undertaking action research. This too shows a level of care. In fact, we could say that 'caring' is one of your educational values, and is already visible. In the next two chapters, we will explore ideas like these further.

In Chapter 1 I am going to guide you through the process of identifying some values for yourself so as to find a research topic. We will examine how it is possible to hold values and yet deny or ignore them in practice. If this is the case it may be giving rise to some tension or concern about your practice. I will describe how this was certainly true for me and how I began to deal with this disquiet.

In Chapter 2 I will show how the concern that I had about my practice was located in the wider conceptual frameworks of care, freedom and justice. Using case studies from my practice I take 'care' as an example and show how I researched the concept in order to get a better understanding of it. I provide you with reflective questions and activities that will help you begin identifying the conceptual frameworks of your study for yourself.

Chapter 1

Identifying an area of professional concern or interest

This chapter explores:

- how articulating your values can help you identify an area of concern in your practice
- how I identified some key questions for myself; for example, 'How do I change what I'm doing so as to transform my classroom from a monological one, where I do most of the talking, to a more dialogical one, where I provide opportunities for my students to talk?'

Identifying an area of concern

Your enquiry into how you can become a better teacher is, perhaps, being driven by a sense of dissatisfaction with some aspect of your practice. As I said earlier, it may be that your values and your practice are in tension. We (you and I) need to establish what might be at the root of that sense of dissonance. This is one of the first steps you need to take in order to develop your understanding of how you might become the kind of teacher you would like to be. We can assume that underpinning your enquiry is a wish to change and improve so as to develop both what you know, and how you teach. Perhaps you also wish to understand more about education in general. Your enquiry will help you to develop a better appreciation of why you do what you do, and how you will learn to do it better. We may well have also identified two more educational values – intellectual curiosity and professional integrity.

If you are reflecting on these matters and are open to the possibility of improvement, then reflection could also be identified as another positive aspect of your professionalism, as could open-mindedness – a core value for improving practice. Dewey (1933) identified open-mindedness, whole-heartedness and intellectual responsibility as qualities of reflective practitioners. I would add intellectual curiosity also. That, after all, is what is at the root of your enquiry.

You will also need to articulate some more of the innate and unnamed values about education that you hold, and the underpinning epistemological and ontological stances that inform them. These terms will be discussed later in greater detail. For now, let us just say that your epistemological stance is to do with how you view knowledge, knowledge generation and knowledge acquisition; your ontological standpoint informs how you view the nature of being – your understanding of *how you are in relation to others*. Identifying and articulating these standpoints will be a key part of your process of self-study action research.

As you embark on your studies you may feel that education is a very complex and political area with many contested terrains and zones of competing interests. In fact you are probably coming to see that your place in the world of education is extremely value-laden. Education is never neutral or value-free – we all have ideas about education and its purposes, although we may not ever have articulated these ideas, even to ourselves. The area of educational research is equally complex and also intricately woven through with a variety of values and assumptions, which again depend on the researcher's epistemological and ontological stances. In later chapters you will be guided through a process of critical interrogation of some of these issues. I will also refer to some of them here.

Being professional involves constantly monitoring one's practice and questioning oneself. Johnson and Golombek state that, for teachers to develop as professionals, there must be 'a process of reshaping teachers' *existing* knowledge, beliefs, and practices rather than simply imposing *new* theories, methods or materials on teachers' (2002: 2). I will now show how I began this process of reshaping my practice for myself. I hope you will be able to benefit from my 'wisdom of hindsight' as I point out some of the big mistakes I made. Here is a synopsis.

A look at my practice

My primary teaching career began in the early 1970s. Starting out I believed that teaching was largely about transmission of knowledge. In the mid 1990s, however, I began to change my practice from a didactic one to a more inclusive and dialogical one that recognised my pupils' capacity for dialogue and critical thinking. I began to study the phenomenon of that transformation in the late 1990s by enquiring into my practice through an action research self-study approach. I changed hugely because of this process of enquiry. I went from being the kind of teacher who followed templates created by others – such as textbooks, worksheets and teacher manuals – to a more creative and autonomous practitioner who took responsibility for how and what I taught (Roche 2011). As I transformed my practice I became a critical thinker, too, helped along by discussions with my students. These discussions were largely based on analyses of children's traditional stories and led me to new and exciting critical engagement with the canon. Because I was studying for my MA by then, I would often present my data in tutorials and the questions asked by my study group and critical colleagues were hugely beneficial in helping me refine and hone my understanding. Likewise, the wise supervision of my tutor was invaluable, as was my reading of critical pedagogy literatures.

Throughout the first part of my career I generally stood at the top of the class and 'talked at' the children. That is what I thought teaching was all about. From the mid 1990s onwards, though, having begun to question my didactic practices, I introduced classroom discussion into my timetable (Roche 2011). Initially these sessions were limited to discussing picture books with my class. As my students and I talked about stories together, I began for the first time to wrestle – along with my 7- and 8-year-old pupils – with questions such as, Was Jack brave or foolish? Was he actually a hero? (Shermis, 1992). What is a hero anyway? Why are the female characters in stories always so passive? Are beauty and docility rewarded by marriage? (Trousdale and McMillan 2003). Were Toad's friends mocking him or mocking his swimsuit? (Lobel 1971). What is friendship? The discussions were amazing and no one was more amazed than me. I realised that I was developing as a critical thinker, helped along by the children in my class.

Suddenly I was questioning everything – institutional practices, uniforms and workbooks, timetables, even the curriculum! And then I realised that the questions raised by our classroom discussions couldn't be corralled any more into one hour per week – they spilled over into every area of the classroom. Children regularly challenged me and each other, courteously and respectfully agreeing or disagreeing or asking for further clarification. It was exciting and my teaching methods were now very different from what I had done before. The dynamic in the classroom was different; it had begun to transform from a monologic classroom to a dialogic one (Roche 2011); my relationship with my students – and theirs with me, and with each other – was different. I was different – and happier.

The process as outlined above seems simple. On the contrary however, it was fraught. Labaree suggests that 'if Sisyphus were a scholar his field would be education' (2006: 77). I frequently felt that I was engaged in rolling an enormous boulder up a hill. How difficult could it be to engage pupils in discussion and critical thinking? It looks straightforward. Comfortingly, Labaree also states that 'teaching is an enormously difficult task that looks easy' (Labaree 2006: 39).

Researching one's practice: self-study action research

Enquiring into one's practice as part of an action research self-study process is grounded in particular values about the nature of knowledge, the nature of research – particularly educational research – and the role of the researcher. As I mentioned earlier, we call these *epistemological* values and you will learn more about this concept in Chapter 4. Your enquiry will also be grounded in *ontological* values. Ontological values are to do with how one sees oneself in the world and in relation to other people. There are many other underpinning values also that may be personal, contextual, institutional and societal, and these values inform who we are, how we are and how we work with others. These too form part of your ontological stance. Always remember that these values evolve and develop along with your understanding.

Let us focus on research briefly. We outlined in the introduction that we locate our methodological framework in 'self-study' action research. This research approach is grounded in ideas that you as an individual can find ways 'to improve your practice and then explain how and why you have done so' (McNiff 2010: 6). It is also grounded in ideas about collaborative enquiry, taking action for improvement, and is open about its value-laden base. Action research is a value-laden form of enquiry (Bassey 1990; Bullough and Pinnegar 2004; Elliott 1991; McNiff and Whitehead 2010; Somekh and Zeichner 2009; Wilcox, Watson and Patterson 2004). It incorporates elements of what Sachs calls 'activism', where teachers develop new understanding and new ways of working with each other and with their communities 'that moves them beyond what have been orthodox forms of association to more progressives and participatory ones' (2003: 4) so as to 'examine the relationship between their espoused theories and their theories-in-use as they define and direct their separate and shared improvement efforts' (2003: 13). There are also elements of what Elliott refers to as 'situational understandings . . . where understanding informs action and action informs understanding' (2004b: 285). This is particularly true for self-study action research, which is about me studying my practice, with a view to improving it – and my understanding of it – and then making that process visible for others (Roche 2011). I am not interpreting someones else's work – I am investigating my own. It is *authentic* professional development. 'Self study allows practitioners to engage in inquiry that contributes to their own capacity for expert and caring professional practice while also contributing to the growth of their professions' (Wilcox, Watson and Patterson 2004: 307). Groundwater-Smith and Mockler suggest that teacher enquiry has five characteristics that could lead to social and educational progress (2009: 13). These are two of them: teacher enquiry is capable of engaging teachers in creating knowledge about and for practice, and it encompasses opportunities for teachers to develop and hone their professional judgement.

Issues to do with action research as a form of educational enquiry will be explained further in later chapters, but for now let us begin by realising that the field of action research differs from other dominant research paradigms in that, at its core, is a *wish to improve* practice, not just to study it. It is a deeply moral endeavour that recognises the uniqueness and dignity of all people. Drawing on Whitehead and McNiff's work we, the authors, understand that rigorous action research is transformative as we seek to establish whether our work has educational influence in our own learning and in the learning or lives of others. We also see that the educational theory that we generate through our research is a 'living' form of theory and in this too we acknowledge the influence of Whitehead and McNiff (2006). Our theories are 'living' in the sense that they are our theories of practice, generated from within our living practices, 'our present best thinking that incorporates yesterday into today, and which holds tomorrow already within itself' (McNiff and Whitehead 2006: 2).

Whitehead and McNiff in turn drew on the work of many other theorists as they honed and refined their ideas. That is part of the excitement of doing educational research. As we reflect on, adapt and hybridise new concepts, we gradually develop our own theories about what we do and why we do it. By reflecting critically on our actions and the reasons for them, we are 'attending to the actualities of our lived lives' (Greene 1988: 7) and engaging in a humanising practice that is fundamental to concepts of democracy and freedom.

As we seek to improve our practice we must be careful to constantly check that what we are doing is for the common good, for a better and more sustainable form of educational practice. This is where practitioner researchers must accept responsibility for the fact that they work with vulnerable others, have the potential for huge influence in the lives of others, and therefore *show* how they ensure that what they are doing is ethically for the good of society (Roche 2011). The showing is important. It can be done as writing up the action report, or by making the research visible in some other public way such as by submitting the written account of the project for accreditation in the academy. McNiff and Whitehead call it 'holding [one's] self accountable' (2006: 34). Such showing also develops teachers' sense of themselves as empowered professionals. Groundwater-Smith and Mockler (2009) suggest that when teachers engage in professional learning that creates authentic knowledge about teaching practice, they are enabled to reclaim their voice in educational discourses and to exercise professional judgement about what constitutes quality in education.

I will use some data and case studies from my own research reports in Chapter 2 to inform and illustrate this idea.

Why did I feel I could be a better teacher? Some background

Ladson-Billings states that 'knowledge emerges in dialectical relationships' and that 'rather than the voice of one authority, meaning is made as a product of dialogue between and among individuals' (1995: 473). Early in my career, I would have had no understanding of what Ladson-Billings meant. My pedagogical knowledge was limited to a very didactic form of teaching, which was at variance with my ontological values about being in relation with others – although I did not have such language at that time. Dialogue with my students was not something to which I gave much thought (see also Roche 2011).

Starting out

In the early 1970s I started out teaching, full of idealism and optimism. Most teachers do, I suspect. Leaving teacher training college, I felt sure that, for the rest of my teaching life, I was going to have happy classrooms full of smiling children, all actively and enthusiastically learning and doing. I saw myself as a kind of 'Maria Von Trapp' figure, with my guitar, my stories and my love of children and excitement at being in their company. I would mould them and shape them into good little happy students, I believed.

It is obvious to me now that my understanding was grounded in some questionable assumptions about teaching, learning, power, relationships, knowledge, freedom, autonomy and motivation. But unaware of all these underpinning assumptions, I felt, starting out, that I was making a difference for good in my pupils' lives and that I would be professionally fulfilled. It is important here to realise that much has since changed in initial teacher training. Contrary to my experience in teacher education, there is now a strong focus on learner-centred pedagogy and reflective practice.

My first experiences in the classroom were traumatic – certainly for me, and, I suspect, equally so for the children. I was 19 years old. I had had two years of teacher education and I had not yet 'become critical' (Carr and Kemmis 1986). I cannot now recall having any participation in discussion about what pedagogy means, or what were the purposes of education. Again, it must be acknowledged that my training took place in the early 1970s and student teachers are now encouraged to engage with such philosophical questions.

My situation was not unusual, I discovered. As part of my doctoral studies, I asked several teachers in various educational contexts if they had ever been given an opportunity to think about, discuss or engage critically with the question 'what is the purpose of school?' when they were students. The responses implied that there was no critical engagement with such questions. In fact, despite being educated in diverse geographical areas (the UK, Ireland, the USA, Canada) the responses were remarkably similar (see Roche 2007: Appendix G, Roche 2011).

I am now working as a teacher educator and I know that student teachers are encouraged to be reflective and to examine their assumptions about education as they develop a personal philosophy of teaching. However, even today there are still some concerns about how student teachers are influenced by an 'apprenticeship of observation' (Lortie 1975) and their own experiences as pupils (Martin and Russell 2009) rather than by what they learn in college. And, unfortunately, it would seem that much of what is observed and experienced is grounded in transmission models and teacher-centred models. Martin and Russell ask:

> How strong is our tendency to think of teaching as a stand-alone activity that occurs independently of learning? How often do we think of teaching as an effort to present information to others with little regard for what they make of it? This restricted view of teaching permeates our culture, created and sustained by our own experiences at school.
>
> (Martin and Russell 2009: 319)

Skamp and Mueller state that teacher educators 'need to be aware that many conceptions held on entry to preservice education may be retained despite methodology units and practicum experiences' (2001: 348).

Alongside concerns about the preconceptions of student teachers is a bigger issue to do with emerging trends in education. There has been much commentary on the culture of 'performativity' that pervades in post-industrial educational contexts (Alexander 2008; Ball 2003; McNamara and O'Hara 2008; Wilkins and Wood 2009). For example, Wilkins and Wood assert that in England performativity has

> created an ethos that encourages compliance rather than critical engagement. In the process, the notion of reflective practice has been diluted, and rather than a genuine engagement with critical issues in professional practice leading to the 'bottom up' development of new initiatives . . . it has come to mean simply assessing the 'effectiveness' of new initiatives by use of simplistic measures of 'what produces better results'.
>
> (Wilkins and Wood 2009: 224–5)

A self-study action research approach will involve thinking critically about such complex issues in education and you will be guided through this process in Chapters 3 and 4.

Reflective activity

It might be helpful for you, now, to ask yourself some more questions to assist you to begin the process of identifying your educational values:

- What answer would I give if I were asked 'what do you believe to be the purpose of education?'
- What has influenced my views?

We will not try to answer these particular questions here. It is important that you continue to revisit them and perhaps develop your ideas as you progress through the book. Your ideas may evolve as you carry out the various reflective activities posed in each section. Elliott states that in learning how to handle the complexity of teaching and learning a 'radical rethinking of the relationship between pedagogy, research and educational policy' (2004b: 286) is needed. 'Radical rethinking' might not be easy and you may need the support of your supervisor and critical colleagues. Wierenga describes how as a PhD student she found the whole field of educational research to be a daunting web of complexity:

> What a shock to find myself in this hazy environment full of conceptualizations and constructs, overlapping but disconnected, with names such as beliefs, intentions, cognitions, principles, orientations, and knowledge that could be formal, situated, personal, or practical.
>
> (Wierenga 2011: 167)

My first teaching experience

Knees knocking and dry throated, I was presented with more than 50 little girls, aged between 4 and 6 years, in a fast-growing school located in a rapidly expanding and socially disadvantaged urban area. The housing complex was architecturally modern, and so was the school. However, my classroom, although bright and airy with up-to-the-minute furnishings, was nevertheless a relic of nineteenth-century schooling: one teacher, no assistant, some 50 plus children.

Teaching these warm and engaging children soon came to be more about control and domination than an enriching teaching–learning experience. I was completely out of my depth. Each night I would look in despair at my lesson plans and fail utterly in my efforts to figure out how to make them meaningful or rewarding. My teacher training had not prepared me for this reality. It never dawned on me to question the social injustice of this situation. It never occurred to me to question why a system of education developed to serve the needs of the Industrial Revolution should still prevail in the late years of the twentieth century (Roche 2011). I did not think about, or know about, the underpinning view of knowledge – the dominant epistemological assumptions – that equated teaching and learning with an 'expert knower' filling 'non-knowers' with 'knowledge'. I was firmly rooted in the idea of a 'teacher-centred' practice. I was unable to differentiate between teacher-centred and learner-centred education.

Reflective activity

Before reading on, see if you can answer these questions, in order to continue the process of reflecting on your educational values:

- What do you consider to be the main differences between a teacher-centred classroom and a student or learning-centred classroom?
- List these differences in columns on a page under the two headings 'teacher-centred classroom' and 'student or learning-centred classroom'.

Now let us check to see if we agree with your replies to these questions.

In a didactic or teacher-centred classroom the understanding is that knowledge is inert – a product that exists 'out there' in books, libraries or the internet – but separate from the knower (see also Roche 2011). The teacher's role is one of domination and control in order to achieve as much coverage of the syllabus as possible. This raises questions about the kinds of teacher–student relationships that are possible in such a classroom. It also raises serious questions about the suitability of a one-size-fits-all national curriculum. (Who decides, for example, what should be known by an 8-year-old and how it should be taught – and why?)

The emphasis therefore is on what the teacher does – which is largely centred on transmitting knowledge. She interprets and mediates and filters her knowledge or the textbook knowledge for the children. The teaching methods are largely didactic in that the teacher instructs and talks *at* the pupils. The students are largely passive – they sit and listen, sit and listen, sit and listen and, when exam time comes, demonstrate 'learning' and 'knowing' by regurgitating what they remember of what they heard. For such passive and silent activity students need to be pliable, placid and obedient. There is little or no pupil dialogue or discussion or activity in such a classroom. Even where there is pupil talk, it is often largely limited to recitation and/or responses to rhetorical or closed 'right-or-wrong' type questions. In such classrooms the teacher is a didact – 'teller' and main talker – and the focus is on what the teacher does as a transmitter of information.

In a child-centred or constructivist classroom however, pupils participate actively in meaning-making – building on existing knowledge so as to make meaning. They are involved in whole class, group and individual work. They argue, debate, discuss and share ideas as they actively construct knowledge for themselves. The teacher's role is that of 'facilitator' in this process and this process demands huge levels of planning, preparation and wide subject knowledge. There is an understanding that the child is a knower and that knowledge is a dynamic process. Objectives are negotiated with the children and authentic deep learning, grounded in curiosity, takes place. A child-centred classroom does not exclude direct instruction. Good teaching will always involve explanation and exposition. The focus, however, remains on pupils' learning, understanding and engagement rather than mere syllabus-content coverage. Qualities such as enthusiasm, passion, curiosity, engagement and enjoyment (the affective domain) are perhaps not easily measured outcomes and so may be forgotten when teachers focus on cognitive domain objectives and learning outcomes for their lesson plans, but I would argue that these same qualities are hallmarks of a learner-centred classroom.

Moving from a monological and didactic practice to one involving constructivist and dialogical pedagogies involved huge amount of reflection for me and the process took a long time.

A reliance on how things were

As you can see, these are complex ideas, which demand critical reflection on the underpinning views of knowledge (which we will discuss in more detail later) so as to better understand the differences between didactic and dialogic constructivist pedagogy. Confronting issues like these and identifying how you stand in relation to them is core to your enquiry. But in my early teaching career, I was nowhere near such critical reflection.

Back to my early teaching experience

In my early teaching experience, falling back on my memories of how things had been for me as a primary school pupil (Lortie 1975; Skamp and Mueller 2001), I completely relied on whole class instruction, and worksheets and workbooks to get through the day. The huge numbers in the class played a role also – but my ignorance of what constituted learning and my uncritical acceptance of didacticism were central features (Roche 2011). Oral work was largely recitation. I shied away from 'scary' concepts like discussion. I aimed for control – control of the children and control and coverage of the syllabus (and of course, what pupils might say in discussion could not be controlled). I had targets but they were *my* teaching targets rather than the children's learning targets. Those little girls were full of patience, tolerance and forgiveness, because I expended huge amounts of energy on keeping the poor mites silent for most of the day. Teacher talk completely dominated my pedagogical approach. Control and domination are key words here.

Let us look at the assumptions here and examine how I appeared to see myself in relation to my students (my ontological values). It would seem that I saw my students as others, 'them', 'the pupils', an homogenous group, out there, separate from me – 'things' to be 'talked at'. Perhaps you can see the assumptions I was then making about knowledge, and knowing and knowers (my epistemological assumptions). It would appear, as I dominated the classroom talk, that I viewed knowledge as a reified 'thing', a product to be delivered or transmitted to 'others'. I can see now, with the benefit of hindsight, that there were also issues to do with my own sense of self, my self-confidence and self-efficacy. Perhaps these were factors also in my bid to maintain a feeling of being in control. Fear was also a factor (Roche 2011: 328). As an unprobated teacher I was constantly afraid of an inspector's unannounced arrival into my room (Jeffrey and Woods 1998).

Reflective activity

Here are some questions for you to think about in relation to your practice:

- How can I ascertain if I value a learning-centred or a child-centred classroom?
- How do I see knowledge – as a product or as a process?

Back to my early teaching experience

I carried on dominating the classroom discourse. The quieter children were invisible to me. I was hugely grateful to them, but I never got to know them. I recognised them as 'good' children.

Reflective activity

Ask yourself:

- What kind of student do I consider to be a 'good' student?
- Why do I think this? Where did I learn this?

Engaging with questions like these is essential for beginning the process of identifying what is your 'epistemological stance'.

Look at the assumptions *I* made. I believed that there was a causal relationship between teaching and learning – 'I've taught it, therefore they've learned it.' I confused being a 'good' teacher with 'doing good' (Bullough and Pinnegar 2009: 246). I thought that 'good' teachers produced 'good' students. I considered a 'good' student to be compliant, passive, invisible, obedient (an assumption about childhood, pupil agency and identity, relationships, power and learning) – who knew the answers to questions (another assumption about the nature of knowledge, what constitutes teaching and the agency, identity and role of teachers).

I only got to know the 'troublesome' little girls who exerted their frustration in attention-seeking and often negative behaviour.

If we consider the assumptions here we might notice that there is labelling, certainly, but far more fundamental issues could include 'othering,' inequity, social justice, care, emancipation, creativity, identity and freedom of expression.

> I soon got a reputation for being 'well able to manage a classroom'. However, despite having acquired this reputation for being a 'good' teacher, deep down, I felt like a complete fraud. It was a gut feeling, a hunch – rather than one grounded in any research or reflection.

Citing Jeffrey and Woods (1998), Ball quotes a teacher:

> You are only seen as effective as a teacher by what you manage to put into children's brains so they can regurgitate in an examination situation. Now that's not very satisfying to one's life. . . . I don't feel that I'm working with the children, I'm working at the children and it's not a very pleasant experience
>
> (Ball 2003: 222)

This sense of feeling like a fraud is perfectly summarised by Whitehead as 'experiencing oneself as a living contradiction' (1989: 42). And this was certainly true in my case.

> As I continued with my teacher-centred practices, I had no idea that, at roughly the same time in Britain, Flanders' (1970) research was causing ripples in the wider education world. Flanders established that, in the classrooms he researched, teacher talk constituted two-thirds of all talk; two-thirds of all the teacher talk consisted of questions posed by the teacher and two-thirds of all the questions were closed questions. The study by Flanders was very large and his findings showed that I was not alone in my didacticism – but at the time I was unaware of this.

This is important. I should have made it my business to keep abreast of new research in education. It is incumbent upon us as teachers to read widely and wisely about our practice (Roche 2011: 328). We will discuss professional reading in more detail later.

I see now that my teaching, and that of many others, was grounded in values of control and domination, and the closing down of freedom of independent thought. Yet we were conscientious, diligent teachers. We tried our best to 'deliver' the curriculum. Because I held values to do with freedom and enjoyment of learning and creativity, I tried to vary my methodologies. But I still dominated the discourse.

I felt frustrated and dissatisfied and I had no idea that I was free to change had I but 'willed' it. Maxine Greene speaks of human freedom as 'the capacity to surpass the given and look at things as if they might be otherwise' (1988: 3). Baldacchino suggests that 'the centrality of Greene's project is that of possibility and choice' (2009: 81). But to be free to change, to avail of 'possibility and choice', you need first to recognise that change is needed, second to have some understanding about *why* change is needed, and third to have some ideas about *how* to change. I did not see, back then, that I had this capacity. I now realise that I did – and you have too.

Professional unease and denial of values

If I were to frame in scholarly language the unease and frustration I experienced, I would state that 'my professional dissatisfaction stemmed from a concern I had that my practice was grounded in a didactic form of pedagogy as I dominated the talk in my classroom'. Perhaps you are getting a sense of how a didactic teaching style is informed by both epistemological values about what knowledge is and how it should be acquired, as well as by ontological values that see pupils as 'them' or 'other' separate from me, not me. Perhaps you see how these underpinning values influence our methodological values – our ways of working and being. I know now that I was uneasy because I realised, at some tacit level, that my values about teaching and learning were being denied (Roche 2011: 329). They were being denied by the wider educational status quo – 'how things are' – but at the same time I was also actively denying my values as I carried out my daily teaching work. I failed to see the children in my classroom as 'people' and, further, I failed abysmally to see those 'people' as individuals. I was a 'living contradiction' (Whitehead 1989).

Like Greene (1988, 2007) my educational values were also grounded in ideas to do with emancipatory practices and social freedom, yet my practice was firmly located in domination and control. I didn't know that bringing about change in myself and in my teaching would demand personal transformation. I didn't yet see that it would involve naming and resisting and overcoming obstacles in order to achieve freedom. It would involve *critical thinking*, which I was not good at doing. It would also involve a sense of *agency*. Agency involves the freedom to make choices about what one does and accepting responsibility for what one does: 'The goal of agency is self-discovery and personal development rather than domination over others, and human interdependency, rather than competition, is stressed' (Parsons 2004: 140).

I was unaware of any sense of agency or autonomy. I stumbled on blindly, feeling my way through the school day slavishly following the textbooks. Then I read Margaret Donaldson's (1978) *Children's Minds.*

Piagetian theory, which suggested that small children could not deal with abstract concepts, dominated my initial teacher education. Now here was Donaldson showing that, contrary to what had been thought (and taught in teacher education courses), children could deal with abstractions. This puzzled me and rattled my convictions about the theory drummed into me in college. McCall (2009) explains how Piagetian stage development theory had a huge influence in informing curricular policy from the 1960s onwards. She suggests that abstractions and ambiguity were written out of curricula as a consequence of the dominance of Piaget's theory, which suggested that children cannot undertake certain tasks until they are psychologically mature enough to do so. It was thought, for example, that young children could not engage in abstract reasoning – so teachers never asked them to try it. I certainly didn't! Years later, though, when I sat and listened enthralled to 4 and 5 year olds discussing what they thought beauty was and what they understood about concepts such as courage and friendship and willpower – as we discussed the stories in Arnold Lobel's (1971) 'Frog and Toad' series – I remembered with shame how I never gave my first pupils the opportunity to engage in such abstract reasoning.

I carried on reading and gradually the questions that I was coming to identify about 'how things were in education' were beginning to gain a clearer focus. Among others, I read John Holt's (1964) *How Children Fail*, Sylvia Ashton-Warner's (1963) *Teacher* and Sybil Marshall's (1968) *An Experiment in Education*. These books inspired me to want to change. I began to seek more books like them. I found Jean Augur's (1986) moving book about her dyslexic sons and felt thoroughly ashamed of all the 'must try harder' comments I had ever written, and I then found Maxine Greene's work and was enthralled (Roche 2011: 330).

A word about professional reading

Cremin *et al.*'s (2009) study on UK-based primary teachers' reading habits showed that many teachers of literacy are themselves keen readers of fiction if not of professional literatures. Rudland and Kemp's (2004: 4) study of Australian teachers shows that professional reading is rare. In the USA, Trelease reports that a study of 224 teachers showed 'they read few or no professional journals that included research' (2007: n/p). More than half had read only one or two professional books in the previous year, and an additional 20 per cent said they had read nothing in the last year. In a survey of 666 academic high school teachers (citing Littman and Stodolsky 1998), Trelease reports that 'almost half reported not reading one professional journal or magazine' (2007: n/p; Roche 2011: 328).

Commenting on the professional reading habits of Irish teachers, Delaney states that Irish teachers have a low level of professional reading – 'the lowest of any participating country . . . this situation may be due to limited access to relevant journals and books rather than a criticism of individual teachers' (2005: 6).

Research, then, would seem to suggest that teachers are not generally interested in reading about education. This is alarming because it is often through reading about the lives of other teachers, or about the profession itself, that a sense of the bigger picture can emerge. This was certainly true in my case. When I read Ashton-Warner (1963) in the early 1980s it had a significant influence in my teaching life. I remember being so enthused by her 'organic' vocabulary that I tried using her methods to improve my teaching of reading.

Reflective activity

Perhaps you could reflect on your own reading now and identify if you have voluntarily read any educational literatures recently, or if your professional literature is limited to required reading or course material. Ask yourself if this situation is of any importance. What might it tell you about your epistemological values?

Let us pause here for a moment and take stock of what has happened so far:

- I experienced a sense of unease about an area of my teaching. This unease was located in bigger issues to do with policy and curriculum, which in turn were underpinned by an epistemology that sees knowledge in a particular way – that decides who is seen as a knower.
- I slowly began to recognise that others are also asking questions.
- I gradually realised that I was not alone in feeling that something was seriously amiss in education. This realisation was perhaps the first paving stone in my path to researching my practice – but I didn't know it then. I did not recognise that identifying my sense of unease was an essential stage in undertaking an action research project. I had not yet asked myself 'What is my concern? Why am I concerned?', which McNiff and Whitehead (2006: 3) identify as the first two steps of an action research plan.

Tacit knowledge and 'gut feelings'

I had never sat down and listed the reasons for my dissatisfaction or unease, let alone problematised or critically encountered them. In my case, I 'just knew' that I wanted my classroom to be the kind of educational space where children could learn through active participation in a community of enquiry, and yet there I was, actively denying those values daily. From my reading I felt that there was a crisis in education generally and I had a hunch that at its core was something about relationships and the way we see ourselves and others. Polanyi (1958) explains how having intuitive knowledge means that we often know far more than we can articulate. I believe that intuitive or personal knowledge – 'just knowing' or having 'a gut feeling' – can be the kind of knowledge that prompts us to take action. In my case, my intuition led me to identify a core dilemma in my practice, between the educational values I held, also intuitively, and my way of working (see also Roche 2011: 329).

> **Reflective activity**
>
> Perhaps you could do that now? Jot down your 'gut feelings' about the things that cause you most dissatisfaction about your work. They may be related to your immediate professional life, your classroom or institution, or the wider educational arena. In the next chapter we will delve more closely into these issues.

Chapter summary

In this chapter we have examined how you can uncover an area of concern in your practice by identifying and articulating some of your core values. I have shown how I identified the question 'how do I change what I'm doing so as to transform my classroom from a monological one, where I do most of the talking, to a more dialogical one, where I provide opportunities for my students to talk'? as a key research area.

Next we will explore how to identify some more core values about education and I will provide a checklist to help you identify stages of the reflective process. Again I will provide some examples from my experience, which you might find helpful for identifying the conceptual frameworks of your study.

Further reading

Some of these books may be out of print but available through libraries and second-hand bookshop.

Ayers, W. (1993) *To Teach: The Journey of a Teacher*, New York: Teachers' College Press.
Includes thought-provoking messages about the vocational aspects of teaching; it invites teachers and teachers-to-be to rethink the project of teaching.
Holt, J. (1964) *How Children Fail*, London: Penguin.
This is an old but still relevant publication. Holt critiques how a focus on 'right answers' can limit the intellectual and creative capacities of children.
Kozol, J. (2007) *Letters to a Young Teacher*, New York: Crown Publishing.
Contains advice for newly qualified teachers about not losing sight of the values that led them to want to become teachers.
Stoll, L., Fink, D. and Earl, L. (2003) *It's About Learning (and It's About Time)*, London: RoutledgeFalmer.
About putting pupils at the centre of the learning process.

Chapter 2

Articulating educational values

Chapter 2 explores:

- how to identify some more core values about education
- how to proceed with the next stages of the reflective process
- how further examples from my experience might help you to discover and name the conceptual frameworks of your study.

Beginning the process of making sense of my practice

When I began teaching I did not have the professional language to frame my ideas. I now know that my educational values were also rooted in values that have their basis in my humanitarian stance – my ontological stance – or how I view myself in relation to others. Perhaps you recognise that although I was motivated in my work by core values of care, compassion and respect for the other, I continued to teach in ways that denied these values. It is hardly surprising that I felt a sense of dissonance. Essentially, the difference between the values I held and the way I behaved towards the children in my class was at the root of my anxiety about my practice. Articulating this took a long time (Roche 2011).

Along with deep and systematic reflection on *my* part it also took the persistent questioning of my research supervisor, who kept on prompting me to articulate my reasons for wanting to change my practice. My supervisor saw, long before I did, that my ontological values were in tension with my lived practices. Wisely, and living to her own values of allowing people freedom to think for themselves, she refrained from telling me. Gradually I began to articulate for myself where my values and my practice were dissonant.

How did I change? Hunches and happenstance

Research often begins with a hunch (DeWalt and DeWalt 2002: 189; Gerrish and Lacey 2010: 14). I would add that research may be triggered by 'happenstance' also.

What was I not doing?

My early teaching was rooted in 'me and my' – *my* lesson plans, *my* objectives, *my* assessments, *my* 'results', *my* classroom. I failed utterly to see that each child also had a right to say 'my classroom'. I knew next to nothing about my students as people. I knew who had 'a reading difficulty', who had 'neat writing', who was 'well behaved', who was 'troublesome' who had 'problems with authority' but very little else.

Your 'happenstance' may have been picking up this book and beginning to reflect on your practice with a view to improving it. However, underlying happenstances and hunches are, perhaps, core educational values. And we need to reflect on them to bring them into the open for ourselves.

Kerry and Wilding suggest that 'reflecting on one's own work can improve one's learning of teaching capability' and they suggest that this is a meta-cognitive process where teachers 'reflect on their own thinking' (2004: 248). As we journey the reflection process together you will see how such a meta-cognitive process can evolve from reflection into action and then into theorising. Theorising involves providing descriptions and explanations of what you do and why you do it. You will need to begin making choices not only to improve your practice, but to examine the options those choices offer before making them. As you take action, you will need to describe and explain your reasons as to why you are making certain decisions (Whitehead and McNiff 2006).

Identifying your core educational values

In Chapter 1 you began to examine some of your core beliefs about knowledge and teaching and learning. This next section will guide you through the process of further identifying and articulating the values that inform how you teach and how you are in your classroom. You will be encouraged to think about the immediate concerns or anxieties you experience in your classroom and how you might locate these in wider conceptual frameworks. You may then consider how you might begin the process of changing.

Some reflective questions to guide you through the process of identifying what might be at the core of your concern

First we focus on the positive aspects. Try to answer the questions below as honestly as you can. After each question I will provide some scaffolding statements and questions to assist you.

What's good about my teaching?
Many teachers enjoy their average school day. Others don't. What do you look forward to? Some teachers are organised and systematic in their approach to planning, teaching and assessment. Some take a more organic approach; they are no less systematic in planning, but are more prepared to go with the flow. What about you?

What do I think are my best professional qualities?
Are they visible in the appearance of your classroom? A teacher's desk can resemble a bombsite – laden with resources, notes, piles of exercise books, workbooks or textbooks. Others' desks can be neat and organised. What about yours? Sometimes children's copybooks reflect a teacher's values. They can be mostly neat or mostly careless and haphazard. The teacher–student relationship may be visible too. For example, do the evaluative remarks you write in feedback show encouragement or disparagement?

You might now be beginning to see that there are some common links. For example, 'my best qualities' may be related to the kind of teacher I am, to my relationships with the children or colleagues – the kind of person I am, or to my classroom atmosphere – the kind of leader, manager and organiser I am.

Now examine what you believe you wish you could *change or improve* about your teaching, your classroom, or your school or education in general. This may have some implications for understanding your own teaching or learning styles, and your strengths and/or weaknesses in learning, teaching and/or managing, as you focus your efforts towards improvement. This may lead to feelings of disequilibrium as some long-held and cherished beliefs are challenged and perhaps cast aside.

Now we will continue with the reflective questions as we look at how some of the areas that you identified above might be located in broader issues.

What's in the bigger picture?

What causes me to feel dissatisfied with my teaching, or to feel that I need to improve either myself or my situation?
For example, your dissatisfaction may be related to a lack of confidence in your teaching skills or competencies. It may have to do with a particular subject area, or an aspect of a curricular area. Your concerns or anxieties may be located at an immediate, practical, pragmatic level, for example thinking about how you can encourage John to do his homework, or help Jane to improve her handwriting. But this concern could also, perhaps, be embedded within bigger issues to do with timetabling, curriculum overload, subject knowledge and/or empowerment. The overriding issue may be to do with dissonance between your epistemological stance and dominant understandings of what constitutes knowledge or knowledge acquisition. There might be underlying issues about learning and control and domination, and social justice. These kinds of matters can become the conceptual

frameworks of your study. By conceptual frameworks I mean the overarching philosophical principles in which we locate our inquiry. Mine were to do with care, freedom and justice. Yours might be different.

How do I discuss or negotiate with my students? If there are sometimes difficulties, is this to do with a particular student or with all my students?
If you are experiencing difficulties then the issue here may be one of fear of loss of control or power (Roche 2011: 336). It may also be to do with how you perceive the role of teacher. Do you see teaching as being to do with transmitting knowledge from an expert, one who knows, to a non-knower? This also has to do with knowledge and epistemological values. It could also be to do with your personal ontological stance.

What about my relationships with my principal or with other colleagues? When do I feel threatened or diminished by others?
The wider issue here might be to do with issues of identity, agency, self-efficacy, power and social justice.

How do I feel about teaching as a life-path or career? Do I believe I am making a difference for good?
These questions may be embedded in wider issues to do with identity or power, or agency. The larger framework here may be to do with ontological values – 'how I see myself in relation to others'.

Perhaps your enquiry into how you might change your teaching is embedded within bigger conceptual frameworks over which you have little or no control – for example, issues such as national policy on curriculum, assessment or school policy (although you may have some educative influence that could lead to institutional change). Perhaps you need to learn ways to work around some systemic barriers. But equally, perhaps, change can also occur in something over which you have some level of autonomy – for example your style of teaching, your collegiality or lack of it, or your style of classroom management.

Now that I have identified some areas of dissonance in my practice how can I change?

The questions above may have offered you some conceptual frameworks in which to locate your study. In my case the frameworks were to do with issues of care, freedom and justice primarily, but these overlapped into concerns about power and control, and I found that as I delved deeper into reading around these areas I grew more and more critical (Roche 2011: 339). I began to change how I *taught*, but this began by changing how I *thought*.

Perhaps before you can implement change in your classroom or in your practice you will need to start with your own thinking. First of all you need to believe that you can change and recognise that the change may begin to evolve even as you take responsibility for reflection. There is a sense of agency in that you are taking control and becoming accountable for what you are doing. Mann refers to 'talking ourselves into understanding' (2002: 195) albeit in a different context.

Here's how I began . . .

Resolving some of the tension

Having identified that I was dominating the discourse in my classroom and that 'too much teacher talk' was at the core of my dissatisfaction, I set about seeking a solution (Roche 2011: 327).

From the middle of the 1990s onwards I began to hold a weekly discussion time based on Donnelly's (1994) 'Thinking Time' model. Donnelly's model was adapted from Lipman's (1982) Philosophy for Children programme and was entitled 'Philosophy *with* Children'. This meant arranging for the children to sit together in a circle, ensuring that they could make eye contact with each other. I sat in the circle as a participant. Rules of behaviour were negotiated together after a few sessions. Topics grew from questions arising from reading a story or a poem, looking at pictures or picturebooks. To begin, a child either volunteered or was chosen at random. This person then had the power to decide whether the discussion went clockwise or anticlockwise by 'passing the tip' (touching the next child lightly on the shoulder). This child then chose whether to speak or to pass. I spoke only when my turn came.

Lest it be assumed that this process happened seamlessly and that the transition from a didactic to a dilaogic classroom was an easy one, I can assure you that it was anything but. The process was fraught with anxiety. I wrestled with questions such as 'Am I wasting time?' 'What will the inspector say if I don't have all the textbooks covered?' 'How do I know that I am doing the right thing here?' Alongside my doubts, the children did not embrace the new practices easily either. They were puzzled by it and did not know what I expected of them. They had become used to what Cazden (1988) called Initiation-Response-Evaluation (IRE) and often sat silently, displaying acute discomfort as I began trying to engage them in discussion. I was working in a 'stuck' school where I was viewed as a person with odd ideas about education (Roche 2011: 330). It was a lonely experience. I frequently felt disgruntled and dismayed, and I vowed many times to abandon the process and revert to whole class didactic teaching. I have outlined in my MA dissertation (Roche 2000) some of the many hiccups there were as I tried to make sense of my 'Thinking Time' sessions.

However, I persevered, initially because I had chosen this area for investigation for my Master's enquiry and professional pride would not allow me to quit. But alongside this there was the nagging certainty that I was living more closely to the values I held (Roche 2011: 330). It is important for teachers engaged in the early stages of research to realise that it can be a lonely and destabilising place.

Mellor speaks of the search for a methodology as a most confusing process:

> I have toyed with the metaphors of a journey . . . and 'hunting the snark', but
> that which most closely embodies the development of this undertaking, with
> its dead ends, confusions, shifts in focus and occasional fruits of publication,
> is the unusual, but nonetheless extremely successful growth of the banyan
> tree.
>
> (Mellor 1998: 467)

Similarly, for much of my study, I had 'no research question and no clear method'. I was 'working without rules in order to find out the rules of what [I]'ve done' (Mellor 2001: 465). Initially I found the situation destabilising because no definitive 'method' exists for self-study action research. I wanted definition, clear answers and a 'right' procedure to follow. I floundered in the methodological freedom I had (Roche 2007: 65).

Bit by bit the children became accustomed to the process and began to look forward to it and to engage more enthusiastically. I found that there were several aspects of this kind of discussion worthy of investigation. There were issues to do with how learners co-construct knowledge and I observed how articulate children scaffolded and supported the less articulate or less confident children (Vygotsky 1962). I began to challenge the unfairness of an evaluation system that labelled children as needing 'remediation' because they did not perform well when it came to pen and paper tests and were, therefore, often positioned as weak or slow learners (Roche 2000, 2011). Yet I could see these same children blossoming when they could display their intelligence through oral language. My data (Roche 2000: 69) showed them as articulate and confident thinkers and speakers.

This led me to read Gardner's book *Frames of Mind* (1983), and as I listened to my pupils discussing and talking I could see how unique each child's intelligence was. I understood now that children make meaning in very diverse ways. I began to provide more time for thinking and talking, and structured my questions in a more open-ended way so there might often be no single 'right' answer, but rather several possible right answers and, possibly, lots more questions. I began to think more deeply about knowledge and knowing. I began to wonder about the kinds of knowing and the positioning of children in relation to knowledge generation. It was all very confusing. *I* needed to think more deeply. This marked a watershed for me as I began to recognise that I held epistemological values that were at variance with the dominant views of what constituted success in a classroom (see also Roche 2011).

I was awakening to the possibility that perhaps there also might be no 'right' answers to many educational questions. I began to reconceptualise the world of school, teaching and learning as a much more complex terrain than I had ever realised. This was destabilising, because I was beginning to discover that the foundations of so many of my assumptions about what constitutes teaching, learning, knowledge, intelligence – even education itself – were not built on the solid rock

I had always envisaged. I experienced the first inklings of a critical interrogation of my previously firmly held assumptions about the status quo of education – 'the way things are'. Critical interrogation is core to self-study:

> Self-study involves using methods that facilitate a stepping back, a reading of our situated selves as if it were a text to be critically interrogated and interpreted within the broader social, political, and historical contexts that shape our thoughts and actions and constitute our world.
>
> (Pithouse, Mitchell and Weber 2009: 45)

We will discuss this in greater detail in Chapters 3 and 4.

It could be argued that initial teacher education prepares teachers better now. As they prepare and teach lessons for their practicum modules, student teachers have a good understanding of different learning styles, and the need to teach for understanding, and the necessity of providing higher-order thinking opportunities through thoughtful open-ended questions. I accept that, but then I must also counter by asking why, if this is the case, is there still a concern about didacticism and dominant teacher talk among educators? For example, Alexander (2008: 117) suggests that the most frequently observed kind of teacher–pupil talk 'still remains closer to recitation than to dialogue'. He says there is a 'need to be honest' about the problems being encountered in attempting to promote a culture of dialogic teaching. Murphy showed that, in the Irish educational context, teachers still dominated the classroom discourse (Roche 2011: 328). He stated that teachers distrusted pupil talk because it distracted from the 'real business of teaching . . . namely listening, reading and writing' (Murphy 2004: 149).

These ideas become embedded in students' minds early. My 8- and 9-year-old pupils loved their discussion times because they felt that 'they're a doss, cos we don't do no work' (sic) (Research diary 13 October 2004). For children, also, it would appear that school 'work' is synonymous with listening, reading and writing. Alexander states that dialogic teaching in British classrooms means, in effect, there is 'a radical transformation of the inherited culture of classroom talk and the attendant assumptions about the relationship of teacher and taught' (2008: 117). Rudduck and Fielding (2006) identified several concerns about 'student voice'. They found that current educational practices and settings greatly underestimate the social maturity of children and young people, and they view this underestimation as a great loss of potential because, they suggest, the gains from including student voice in meaningful decision making can have a significant positive impact on students' academic, social and personal development.

Dewey (1916) saw schools as mini-societies and argued that in a progressive democratic society the education system would need to prioritise making provision for experiences where children could develop the habits of critical thinking and the democratic skills and dispositions that they would need as adults.

Reflective activity

This activity focuses on issues that were relevant for me. Even if these questions do not have much relevance for you, perhaps you can use them as examples of the kinds of questions that will help you to move your enquiry along. Think about your classroom and the most recent lesson you taught. Ask yourself:

- Who did most of the talking? What about 'real' talking by the children? How can I tell the difference between dialogue, and merely giving children time for extended answers (Alexander 2008)?
- What role do students have in decision making in my classroom or in my school? How often are their voices listened to? What change happens as a result of suggestions made by students? What is the balance of power in classroom talk?
- What issues do I need to address so as to provide children with time for thinking?
- How do I ask questions in class? What feedback do I give to the answers pupil provide? Could it be that although I give my pupils time to think, and space to provide an extended or fuller answer, the answers that count are still those that I want or expect?
- If students appear to be seeking to provide me with the answers they think I wish to hear, rather than engaging with authentic thinking for themselves, what does this show me about my, and their, epistemological stances?

Critical interrogation: underlying assumptions that need to be challenged

When I reflected on what I was doing to provide more opportunities for authentic talking and thinking, I saw that I needed to look at issues to do with power, at the freedom children had to speak or not speak, and at silence. Examining the power of silence was very interesting (Rice and Burbules 2010). Didactic teaching *demands* silence. But in a classroom discussion setting, do we *allow* silence? What does the silence of a child say? If a child remains silent when asked a direct question in a didactic classroom setting, an assumption might be made that the child does not know the answer, is being defiant, is inattentive or cannot hear properly. In a discussion setting silence – or passing the 'tip' – by a child can mean that the child is still formulating thoughts, or is not ready to speak, or is having a little day-dream, or is too busy listening and thinking to speak. The idea of teacher silence – or lack of it – presents different questions. Quite often, when I looked at videos following discussions, I was horrified to see that I was still dominating the discourse by the leading questions I asked, or by my negative body language when children said things I didn't agree with.

As I continued to examine my practice, I also found the critique of my study group invaluable as I sought to improve what I was doing. I would present pieces of data and my colleagues would challenge and question my work. More importantly, my tutor's support was invaluable as she probed and prodded me into providing a rationale for what I was doing. Her persistent question was: why *are you doing what you are doing?* In searching to come up with honest answers I found myself trying to work out my personal philosophy of education. Reading Burbules' article 'The Dilemma of Philosophy of Education' (2002) also raised my awareness of the relevance of engaging with the philosophy of education.

This is where it might be helpful for you to identify a colleague who would agree to be a 'critical friend' – someone who would help you to be reflective about your teaching. Perhaps together you could now begin to articulate the first elements of your 'personal philosophy of teaching'. Bear in mind that this may evolve.

As my study progressed, issues arose that were to do with the curriculum and how it is designed, delivered, and interpreted or implemented in a large school (Roche 2011: 329). I began to critique the busy-ness of the school day – the 'hurry-along curriculum' (Dadds 2001). It seemed that, through encouraging children to think critically, I too was 'becoming critical' (Carr and Kemmis 1986).

How do I know that I am right?

One of the questions that you must ask yourself as you plan for or carry out your research is: 'How do I know that what I am doing is right?' You might feel that, because you have examined your teaching to see in which area you feel a sense of dissatisfaction or dissonance, and have begun to put in place some strategies for improvement, that automatically you are 'right'. But how can you be sure? You might argue, 'I'm trying to live more closely to the values I hold. Surely that must be a good thing to do?' I could reply that some of the worst and cruellest dictators lived to their values. Many articulated their values in writing and put them into the public domain. We must assume that they thought they were 'right'. We need to establish somehow that what we are doing is for the benefit of others (Whitehead and McNiff 2006). What checks and balances can we put in place to ensure that our improved practice is sustainable, life-affirming, for the betterment of others – for the common good? How can we be sure that we are having an educative influence in the lives of others?

McNiff, Lomax and Whitehead maintain that professionals can influence others in ways that are educative or in ways that are destructive. If relationships with external others are 'grounded in commitments to freedom for all to learn and grow' (2003: 48), then professionals are more likely to act in educative ways that benefit the participants. They will be open and honest with all research participants. They will inform participants about what they (the professionals) are doing and gain their voluntary consent. By constantly revisiting our values, by holding these values as the open and accountable standards of judgement (Whitehead and McNiff 2006) against which we test our claims to knowledge, we are all the while checking to see if we are living our articulated values in our daily practice.

Hartog (2004) establishes how she tests her claims to be working in an ethical way. She asks:

> Are the values of my practice clearly articulated and is there evidence of a commitment toward living them in my practice?
>
> Does my inquiry account lead you to recognise how my understanding and practice has changed over time?
>
> Is the evidence provided of life-affirming action in my teaching and learning relationships?
>
> Does this thesis evidence an ethic of care in the teaching and learning relationship?
>
> Are you satisfied that I as researcher have shown commitment to a continuous process of practice improvement?
>
> Does this thesis show originality of mind and critical thinking?
>
> (Hartog 2004: 3)

Hartog's thesis on ActionResearch.net (<http://www.actionresearch.net>) and our work with Educational Action Research in Ireland (<http://www.eari.ie>) show the efforts people have made to establish if what they were doing was educative. Lomax defines an 'educative' relation as 'includ[ing] the idea that there will be learning and improvement (change) that involves both the self and others independently and reciprocally' (2000: 51).

Reflective activity

Ask yourself:

- What steps can I take to ensure that what I am doing will be for the betterment of others?
- How can I determine that my research will have an educative influence on my own learning and in the learning of others?

To return to my classroom situation

My pupils now loved their weekly 'Thinking Times'. They frequently chose the topics for discussion, and as they became more proficient at dialoguing with each other, I gradually began to realise that this work was transformative. It had profound effects in the classroom.

I noticed a new kind of relationship forming between my pupils and me, and between them and each other. My classroom discussions were not intended to be about behaviour modification, like Mosley's *Quality Circle Time in the Primary Classroom* (1998). Raising test scores was not an objective either. I simply wanted to provide opportunities for us to engage in dialogue together. I timetabled it in my planning notes as 'English: Oral Language'. But I soon saw that it was much, much more. The children seemed to trust me more and I got to know them as individual people. Their insights about stories and their articulation of them delighted me.

Let us examine what was happening simply because I tried to live out my values in my practice and then reflect on them (see also Roche 2011). Both of these aspects are important – the actual practice and the reflection.

I began to see my students in a different light. Hearing them articulate their ideas, opinions and thoughts was transformative for me because they ceased being just 'pupils'; instead they became for me 'the people I worked with'. They seemed kinder, more tolerant and more open with each other – more ready to see others' points of view outside the discussion time. I felt that they began to see me as a person too. The process spread from my classroom: A teacher from a neighbouring urban disadvantaged school observed some discussions and soon began holding them with her own class. She too found the process transformative:

> The empathy engendered by Mary's version of classroom discussion permeates the children's way of being with others and colours their interpersonal relationships at class and whole school level. Teachers have commented on the maturity and kindness of my girls. I feel the girls learn self-respect and respect for others and learn to see me as a human being, capable of feelings, as opposed to being 'just a teacher'.
> (Roche 2007: Appendix B2)

Along with the many significant improvements at the affective level, I observed several cognitive benefits. Because our discussions were often centred on stories that I read aloud, I noticed improved critical literacy in the class generally. With their honed critical thinking powers, my pupils – 6- and 7-year-old boys – began to challenge stereotypes and norms: they began to disagree with me about 'what the author meant'; their higher-order thinking abilities became more obvious as they became more articulate. Children who had been labelled as poor readers frequently demonstrated more critical discernment than their more literate peers

(Roche 2000, 2007). Trickey and Topping (2004) refer to cognitive improvements in Scottish children who engaged in classroom discussion, and the work of Fisher (1990), Haynes (2002), Murris (2000) and McCall (2009) found philosophical classroom discussion similarly transforming.

The most important finding for me was the realisation that, through holding classroom discussions, I was moving from a teacher-centred practice towards a more child-centred practice, which was in harmony with my ontological stance. Reflecting on my work and engaging in self-study action research around it was beginning to have a profound significance for how I articulated my values and worked towards realising them (Roche 2011).

Looking at some bigger issues: examining my ontological values

In the previous chapter I outlined how, although I valued a child-centred classroom, I continued to work from a teacher-centred pedagogy. Now, through reflection and through discussion with my supervisor and critical friends, I was slowly realising that these ideas were located in some much wider conceptual frameworks of care, freedom and justice. It took a long time to arrive at these conclusions. But having identified that these key ontological values were informing my personal educational values, I saw that I needed to interrogate these concepts further because I felt they were core conditions for the development of dialogic and democratic pedagogies.

Gradually I also came to understand that by encouraging my students to discuss and develop their considerable power for thinking for themselves, I could actually realise these values in my day-to-day work (Roche 2011). But I was doing the work for quite a long time before I began to be comfortable with the interrogation of these values. I needed huge amounts of reading and reflection before I began to make changes to my practice. Then I took some action, and as I reflected on what I did, I saw that I needed to examine what were the conceptual frameworks, or the guiding principles, that informed my actions. This led me to study literatures to do with 'othering'.

In previous pages, I showed how I came to recognise the children I worked with as individuals through dialoguing with them. I had shifted from seeing them as a generic bunch of 'pupils' – the 'abstract and generalised other' – to seeing them as 'real and concrete other[s]' (Benhabib 1987). This had profound influence now in how I planned lessons, how I chose resources, how I taught (Roche 2011: 340). It was grounded in ideas of 'care' first of all. This was also a first step towards articulating my ontological stance. Let us now look at the concept of care.

Examining the concept of 'care'

I researched literatures on care and caring because I wanted to explore how I understood the concept in relation to my work. In the literature, caring has been described as a fundamental human capacity that translates into a coherent pattern of behaviours in life affirming interpersonal interactions (Iaani 1996; Noddings 1992). I learned that caring sees the creation of trusting relationships as the foundation for building an effective academic and social climate for schooling (Erickson 1993). Lin suggests that caring may not be visible or explicit in an educational environment, 'yet it guides the interactions and organization of schools and classrooms' (2001: 2).

Reflective activity

Let us assume that care is one of your conceptual frameworks. You would now need to reflect on some questions about care:

- What are things I care most about in teaching?
- What do my school management team and staff appear to care about?
- What values of care are reflected in my school's policies or appearance?
- What have I learned from carrying out this activity?

Inspired by conversations with my supervisor and study group, I began to question the idea of how values are often positioned in dominant literatures as abstract linguistic phenomena rather than living practices. My understanding is that values need to transform into lived practices if they are to have meaning in the social world (Raz 2001). This idea is well developed in the work of McNiff (e.g. 2006). I came to see that values need to be examined from the perspective of seeing other people as 'concrete others' (Benhabib 1987). I needed to relate my values to the real individuals in my classroom. I began to understand 'care for others' as 'care for real others' (Roche 2011: 340).

Reflective activity

As I show you some vignettes from practice now, see if you agree that I began to live my value of care in my classroom.

Living values in practice – two case studies
(Names have been changed to protect anonymity.)

Charlie's story
In 2001 I had a class of 27 mixed gender junior infants (4–5 year olds). The children were generally very well behaved (in the normative understanding

of that term) apart from Charlie. Charlie appeared to hate fine motor activities and whenever they began, he would walk about, open cupboards and act in a mildly disruptive way. I introduced class discussion, and, one day, following a story from Fisher (1996) I asked the children for their thoughts about the concept of beauty. I noted that nearly all the children articulated beauty by describing something concrete and visual. Then Charlie suddenly announced from outside the group that he 'knew what the most beautiful *sound* in the world was'. I was amazed that he was paying this much attention.

What Charlie actually said was:

> Teacher, if you were all alone in a deep dark forest and if there was all shadows everywhere and you were really, really scared, and then if you heard a voice saying 'Charlie . . . It's Mummy, I'm over here . . . . Wooo! THAT would be the most beautiful sound in the world!'
>
> (Research diary, 19 December 2001)

As he spoke he fixed his large, intelligent grey eyes on mine. I was moved by what he said and by his earnestness, and I believe I communicated that to him without making any overt value judgement. (During classroom discussions I try to refrain from passing any comments that place me in too much of a teacher or authority role, preferring to participate at the level of person-in-the-circle.) I felt that he *knew* I was moved and that I was pleased he had joined the group. This episode marked a kind of watershed for Charlie, because although he remained restless and needed to walk around a lot, he consistently showed that he had considerable verbal reasoning skills and became a consistent contributor to discussions.

Alex's story

In another junior infant class Alex was another restless boy, but unlike Charlie he showed it in noisy and assertive ways. He often disrupted other children's work causing them to complain. As before, I introduced my classroom discussion programme. I chose as a topic the question, 'What would happen if you left your teddy out in the rain?' I was also trying to 'cover' some of the syllabus. The topic was an activity suggested by some oral language development cards from my English syllabus, and it had the aim of developing the children's competency to use words to describe 'wetness'. However, my research diary notes show that the dialogue went far beyond describing 'wetness':

> Emma: Your teddy might get robbed if you left it out all night.
> Alex: I know how to catch a robber. See, you dig a hole, right? And you put a blanket over it and then put some dirt on the blanket and the

robber won't see it and he'll step on it and fall into the hole. That way you'll get your teddy back and then you could call the police and they'd take him away.

(Research diary, 16 February 2003)

I realised that Alex had a theory about catching robbers. He had provided a description of a 'robber trap', followed by an explanation of how it would work. I was excited by this idea and began to look out for more examples. I realised the children had lots of theories about the world and how it worked; see 'transcripts' in Roche (2007: Appendices). I began to reconceptualise my young pupils as theorists and co-constructors of knowledge. I also began to interrogate some classroom norms.

Alex contributed several more times to the discussion and clearly enjoyed himself. At the end he asked, 'When can we do that again?' He had been given a chance to 'shine' through participating in discussions that afforded him the opportunity to demonstrate his excellence in talking and thinking. I encouraged caring and just behaviours in these discussions. For example, I introduced the children gradually to the language 'I agree with X because . . . and I disagree with X because . . .'

Looking at Charlie's and Alex's stories as reflective learning opportunities

These two episodes were significant learning experiences for me. In Charlie's situation, I realised that the conventions of a junior infant (4–5 year olds) classroom seemed to place extraordinary emphasis on stillness and conforming and compliant behaviour. As I discussed in the previous chapter, children who exhibit these qualities are often positioned as 'good' children. For instance, Charlie had been described as 'messy' and 'disruptive' in a previous teacher's notes to me. Two teachers had labelled Charlie 'disruptive' but had not made any reference to him being intelligent, articulate, logical and witty, or a good listener. However, through implementing a more dialogical practice, I now saw that he exhibited keen critical thinking abilities and I noted that he 'questioned a lot'.

Charlie's questions were transformative for me. I now began to question systemic norms, too, and his challenges led me to critique my own practice even more (Roche 2011). Now I started searching for teaching strategies to support the kind of enquiring mind that Charlie had. Despite having read Gardner's (1983) theories of multiple intelligences I had regressed into treating the class as a unit. Now I created opportunities for the children to learn through enquiry. I encouraged them to work collaboratively and I had them out of their seats and out of doors as much as possible. I was slowing creating a more learner-centred pedagogy.

At four and a half years of age, and the youngest child in the class, Charlie wanted answers to several critical questions:

- Why do we have to do homework?
- Why do children have to go to school at all after they have learned to read?
- Why does everybody in the school have to wear blue except the grownups?

If I gave him an answer that made sense to him he accepted it; if not he stared at me and said 'Yeah, OK' and walked away, clearly disgruntled. (Research diary, 21 November 2001)

Alex's imaginative and problem-solving response made me question what Dewey might have called an 'anaesthetic' prescribed syllabus that assumed children would answer questions about a teddy left in the rain in a predictable way and would therefore be led towards developing a vocabulary of 'wetness'. There seemed to be no understanding that a small child could generate questions and provide hypotheses. I saw now that I needed not only to provide talking opportunities, but that I also needed to listen carefully to my pupils.

Reflective activity

Ask yourself:

- What assumptions were likely to have been made about these little boys if they hadn't been provided with opportunities to demonstrate their considerable thinking powers?
- How do you provide individual students with opportunities that allow their different abilities to shine?
- What did I learn from Charlie's critical questions and Alex's robber-catching theory?

When I reflect on my actions, I realise that it was my regard for Charlie and my values of care that influenced me. I see now that there were several issues involved, several sets of values to do with freedom and respect, and power too. But care was core. I did not force him to conform: I respected him and he responded well to that care and respect. Likewise, with Alex, I saw that I needed not only to provide him with opportunities to display his knowledge orally but also that I needed to provide him with 'real' authentic problem-solving scenarios.

For Noddings (1984), caring for others involves an act of transcendence. For me, it certainly involved transcending my own classroom management needs for, perhaps, order and quiet, in order to meet the needs of those with whom I was in a caring relationship. It meant learning to accommodate children who wished to remain silent in our discussion circles, or who did not wish to participate in the circle; it involved a kind of reaching out towards others. Care, according to Noddings (1984), can involve the gift of being able to see the infinite beauty and uniqueness of the other as a complete human being equal to ourselves. This then is where I see my ontological values meeting my epistemological values and transforming into living methodological values.

Reflective activity

Now ask yourself these questions and check if your answers relate to the values you articulated earlier:

*   When I am planning lessons how do I plan with the whole class in mind?
*   How do I plan lessons so as to offer learning opportunities that suit the needs of individual children? (Do I even *know* their individual learning styles?)

In the same way as I interrogated the concept of care and how it related to my practice I also researched the concepts of freedom and justice. This involved a lot of reading, reflecting and discussion with colleagues and critical friends. Relating my values of freedom and justice to real and concrete others meant that I began to recognise that such values were centred on my concern that an education that denies the capacity of children such as Alex and Charlie to think for themselves, and to demonstrate their abundant gifts and abilities, is unjust and uncaring. I saw that an element of what Noddings (1984) calls 'I ought' is present therefore. Because I am their teacher, with what I believe is a moral obligation to try to provide the children with the best education possible, I have a moral responsibility to examine my values keenly and seek to live towards them (see also Alexander 2008: 183; Roche 2011).

I could now demonstrate that I was trying as far as possible to meet the emotional as well as the academic needs of my students. They responded well in turn to feeling cared for. In Charlie's case I felt I got to know *him* when he said that he 'actually knew' what the most beautiful sound in the world was. In Alex's case it was when he presented his theory of catching robbers; in other classrooms it was when Sarah explained what she thought 'commoners' were, Max told me about the 'smell' of the ladybirds in his garden, James explained about spiders eating their own webs for 'a bit of nourishment', Owen told me about his cat 'making plans' and Aoife told me 'when you get an answer you can always question the answer' that I got to know these children as the warm lovable caring people with whom I love working. (These episodes are all documented in Roche 2007; see also Roche 2011.)

My capacity for silence

I started out on this odyssey of self-study in order to move from a didactic practice to a more dialogic one. The video evidence I presented with my thesis in 2007 showed that I rarely speak during class discussions except at the beginning of the discussion period. I had to reflect on the importance of my silence in classroom discussion (see Rice and Burbules 2010). Fiumara speaks about the silence of listening as 'the other side of language' (1990: 4). By staying silent in classroom discussions as much as possible, I can use my silence to provide opportunities for my students to find their voices and think and speak for themselves.

Quests for meaning

When I read Maxine Greene's (1978) argument that unless educators engaged in their own quests for meaning they would be unlikely to be able to influence or encourage others to do so, it made sense to me (Roche 2011: 330). Through reading the work of Greene (1988) I was helped to understand for myself what an 'education for freedom' might involve. I began to formulate my own ideas. I understood that educating for freedom meant that I would have to endeavour to change. I saw that I would need to encourage myself (alongside, and in relation with, my students) to come to an awareness of the many points of view there can be of every situation, and the multiple ways that exist for interpreting our worlds. I reflected on what freedom meant in my classroom and came to the conclusion that to be free is to be able to think and speak for oneself; to be able to engage the world in an ongoing conversation; and to value the power and meaning that new points of view may bring to the collective search for fulfilment (Roche 2007: 106).

Learning to learn, learning to question, to reach out, and to draw relationships between my values and my practice became a key focus of my research and informed my conceptual frameworks. It led to huge transformation in my way of being in my classroom with my students and in my way of thinking about education. It influenced the practice of colleagues and led to the formation of a school-wide policy and practice also (Roche 2011: 338). From those early tentative enquiries into my practice I arrived at a point where a practice that I had introduced to my school was singled out for comment as a school-wide practice during a whole school evaluation report:

> Pupils in the senior classes display a growing competence in presenting and supporting arguments and in speaking articulately. The implementation of thinking time to further develop pupils' critical thinking skills is a notable feature of all classroom practice and merits high commendation
>
> Ireland, DES (2009: n.p.)

Conclusion

You have begun the process of articulating your values and identifying an area or areas of concern about your practice. Now you need to do some hard work: you need to reflect vigorously on what might be the conceptual frameworks of your study and begin to research them. Mine were care, freedom and justice, and I read widely around these topics. Reading is essential. It will help you form a basis from which you can challenge your thinking and actions.

Chapter summary

This chapter has explored addressed issues to do with *what* might be areas of concern. In the next part of the book you will be introduced to several more critical interrogations of educational norms as you address issues around *why* you might have concerns.

Never underestimate what you might achieve by reflecting on your practice, and identifying some areas of dissonance between the values you hold and the way you work (McNiff 2010: 258, Roche 2011: 338). Self-study action research by you, on you, has the potential to transform your way of working, thinking and being. It also has the potential to influence others in ways you cannot yet imagine.

Further reading

Some of these books may be out of print but available through libraries and second-hand bookshop.

Darder, A., Baltodano, M. and Torres, R.D. (eds) (2003) *The Critical Pedagogy Reader*, New York and London, RoutledgeFalmer.
   Introduces key critical issues in contemporary education.
Greene, M. (1988) *The Dialectic of Freedom*, John Dewey Lecture Series, New York: Teachers College Press.
   Examines the relationships between education, freedom, possibility and imagination.
Noddings, N. (1992) *The Challenge to Care in Schools: An Alternative Approach to Education*, New York: Teachers College Press.
   Examines the concept of care from moral and ethical perspectives.
Pollard, A. (ed) (2008) *Readings for Reflective Teaching*, London and New York: Continuum.
   Summarises several key educational literatures.

Part 2

Critical thinking about practice

Máirín Glenn

In this part I will take the ideas outlined in Part 1 and develop them. I invite you to question the reasons for your educational concerns and to reflect on the work of Jack Whitehead (1989) as you explore questions like 'Why am I concerned?' and 'Why am I interested in my work?' In this phase of your research, you may begin to develop ideas around how you might improve your practice or your understanding of it. This is one of the initial stages of the process of generating your educational theory from your practice – a process which will be outlined in the course of subsequent chapters.

In Chapter 3 I talk about how you might reflect on and develop a better understanding of your practice. I describe how self-study action research is frequently not a linear process and that it often can become quite 'messy' and complex. I introduce the idea of the role of reflective practice in practitioner research in the classroom. I outline how a reflective journal can enhance the reflective process and emphasise the importance of critical thinking. I discuss the idea of informed committed action as praxis, show the importance of focusing the research on oneself along with others, and explore how you can 'step back' from your work and develop a new awareness of what is happening in your everyday work. I point out the importance of engaging with literature, not only in your focal area but also in a broader context.

In Chapter 4 I take the idea of thinking critically a step further and explore ideas around how educators can experience themselves as a 'living contradiction' (Whitehead 1989). I show how the space between the values educators hold for themselves and what they actually do in practice can be the kernel to how they research their practice. I examine ideas around critical pedagogy and give an example from my work in the classroom to demonstrate the relevance of critical pedagogy for educators. To conclude, I draw up a model that you may find useful for exploring how you might interrogate why you are concerned or have questions about your practice.

Chapter 3

How can I develop a better understanding of my practice?

This chapter explores:

- the role of reflective practice in practitioner research
- how a reflective journal can enhance the reflective process
- the importance of critical thinking.

Introduction

When practitioners undertake research into their own practice and seek to improve aspects of that practice or to improve their understanding of it as they seek to generate new theory (McNiff and Whitehead, 2009), one step they take is to identify an area of professional concern or interest. In the previous part of the book we outlined how this process might be undertaken. This area of professional concern may be causing anxiety for the practitioner or it may be an area that the teacher feels needs some investigation, or indeed it can be an area that the teacher feels should be celebrated. A closely related phase of the research process seeks to identify *why* this issue is of concern to the practitioner (see Whitehead and McNiff 2006) and this is the phase that will be discussed in this chapter.

Establishing why an issue is of concern or is attracting your attention usually involves some deep reflection on the chosen area of interest. It also calls for critical thinking on the part of the practitioner and sometimes requires them to 'dig deep' into their beliefs and everyday practices. Moon (2004: 100) explains that in-depth reflection is characterised by an 'increasing ability to frame and reframe internal and external experience with openness and flexibility'. In this chapter I will build on the ideas in the previous chapters and explore my own reframed experience of critical reflection. I will draw on examples from my experiences in my practice as a teacher to illuminate these issues. I will outline my professional concerns and questions, my investigation of them and the difficulties I encountered in the process. I will describe how, when I interrogated my area of professional concern, I asked questions like 'Why am I concerned?', as suggested by Whitehead and

McNiff (2006). I will also outline the learning journey I undertook to tackle questions like 'Why do I do what I do?' and 'How can I develop a better understanding of my work?' I will help you to focus on your own area of interest and to think critically about it by sharing some of the questions that I posed for myself.

Taking a research journey: complexities and messiness

As you undertake your research project and begin to plan it, you may feel that sometimes your research is not going to plan. You might have read about the 'research journey' or 'research stages' but you might feel that finding a starting foothold is difficult, and that taking a 'journey' seems impossible. The metaphor of a research journey might be a little misleading because it could lead you to believe that action research is a nice, neat, linear process. Very often, this is not the case. Frequently research can be a messy and non-linear process. Mellor (2001) talks about 'the struggle' and explains how his struggle in his practice and research was at the heart of the research and that the struggle became the methodology itself.

Clandinin, Downey and Huber (2009), who work in the area of narrative inquiry, use the metaphor of a landscape to describe the professional work of teaching, and they refer to the complexity of the multi-layered professional lives of teachers, where moral, historical, personal and epistemological worlds merge. Education can be 'messy' work and educators often find themselves juggling those 'worlds' as they try to ensure that they are providing a balanced educational environment for their students. Crowell seems to echo the sentiments of Clandinin, Downey and Huber as he suggests the metaphor of a tapestry: 'Who I am and how I teach is woven together by the tapestry of my life's experiences and, I believe, by the ultimate quality of my commitments' (2002: 14). In my teaching and researching experience, if I were to make a tapestry of the story of my research into my own practice, the loose ends would never be tidied away neatly; they would frequently be unfinished and sometimes unravel because they reflect the complexity of a lived reality. As an action researcher, I look upon each ending as a new beginning, with a new set of concerns. McNiff and Whitehead call this the 'paradox of the ideal' where 'we imagine the way things could be, but as soon as we have an answer, new questions arise' (2010: 108). Regardless of which metaphor suits your needs, it is important to remember that action research into your practice is frequently not linear and that, sometimes, solutions or insights are not always apparent. Your learning – your insight into your work and the generation of theory from your work – is not always immediate either. It may take place weeks, months or even years after the event from which it originated, and in a reflective moment, a new insight into an old dilemma might suddenly emerge. Sometimes, you do not achieve clarity; instead, you generate more questions!

In these chapters, as we examine why we might have specific concerns or areas of interest in our work, it is important to remember also that one stage of the research does not always follow neatly on from the previous stage. Some researchers find it more helpful to query *why* they are concerned before they can actually pin down *what* their area of concern might be. This might be a useful strategy for you. Action research is a series of never-ending spirals (see McNiff and Whitehead 2009) and sometimes what appears to be the beginning is actually a mid-point, and what appears to be the end is actually a new beginning.

I will now draw on an experience from my practice as a primary level teacher to highlight the complexities I encountered in the process of engaging in research into my own work.

Why do I do what I do?

I was teaching in a very small rural primary school on the west coast of Ireland and some years ago, when digital technology was becoming more readily accessible for educational purposes, I found myself drawn to it. I liked to experiment with it in my homework and found it to be an exciting new way to work with children. I liked the way multimedia helped children whose learning strengths were not of a mathematical or linguistic nature to find confidence in expressing their learning. Difficulties with writing and reading seemed to be less significant when a computer was involved. The students liked the idea of having a worldwide audience when they published their work on the web and this encouraged them to write. When we engaged in communication projects with schools in far-flung lands, I felt that even though we were geographically removed, we were just a mouse-click away from e-pals on the far side of the globe.

I was so animated by these ideas that I undertook a Master's degree to further my understanding of how technology might help my teaching and learning. In the process of my studies, I read widely around the literature that was current at that time. Much of the literature supported my thinking and my ideas around the possible uses of technology in school. I delighted in the fact that I seemed to be engaging in what seemed to be 'good' practice, according to the literature.

However, as I subsequently began to reflect on my practice a little more carefully, I realised that, despite my reflection about my work and my use of technology to enhance teaching and learning, I had never asked myself in any detail, 'Why am I doing this?' I had somehow decided that if the literature at that time supported the practices with which I engaged, then my work must be 'good'. However, this did not provide an answer to questions like 'Why am I doing this?'

The focus of my research was on my use of digital learning as a classroom teacher. As I worked through the processes that Mary outlined in Chapters 1 and 2, I found that much of my professional thinking lay with my work with technology in education. I knew that, at the time, my work was fairly innovative and interesting, but I was not sure how or why I was concerned about my work. I also found it difficult to articulate what my values were. I became frustrated and I drew comfort from Mellor's writing as he describes the struggle he had while researching his practice:

> I know I have a goal, which is that I want to look at my job but I don't know what the questions are to ask but I will know when I get there. . . . It is only by getting stuck in and . . . being confused and asking questions: What am I doing? Why am I doing it? that it becomes clear.
>
> (Mellor 1998: 454)

As I explored my work and reflected on it carefully, I realised that a gap existed somewhere within my knowledge. Before I could engage with my research, I needed to clarify what my values were and I needed to be able to articulate why I was concerned about my work. I now know, as I look back, that my new work practices with technology were an expression of my ontological and epistemological values. I also know that although I was acting out my values in my work, I was doing this in an unknowing and uncritical manner. I can see now that I was developing my technology projects more from an intuitive perspective than from a position of critical thinking. At that time, I was frustrated with my lack of insight into my practice.

As I strove to develop a clearer understanding of my work, I realised that my work practices had changed. I had changed from being a 'regular' didactic-style teacher to someone who had begun to give children the opportunity to think for themselves, to take charge of their own learning – to a certain extent at least – and to use more digital learning in my work so as to allow this opportunity to arise. As I gradually became aware of this change in my work I also was exploring ideas around reflective practice and self-study action research. I found that I was concerned about my lack of understanding around these new work practices. I found that while I was able to describe my work well, I was unable to offer adequate explanations around it.

Reflective activity

Ask yourself:

- Why do I do what I do in my everyday practice in the classroom?
- Why am I concerned about certain aspects of my work?

Developing insights and understandings: thinking critically

Slowly the fog of confusion lifted and some clarity entered my thinking. My reading of relevant educational literature and my serious engagement with it helped, as did the gentle prodding from my tutor, Jean, who asked me questions like: 'What is the benefit of locating communities in cyberspace?' and 'Why do you want to encourage people to share their ideas?' This is very important, and central to what you are trying to do. Let us try and work out why you want to encourage people to share their knowledge and how technology can do that.

I experienced great difficulty in answering these questions and in articulating why I changed my everyday teaching habits. Polanyi outlines personal or intuitive knowledge as being a valid form of knowledge: 'We can know more than we can ever tell' (1967: 4). He called this pre-logical stage of knowing 'tacit knowledge'. He continues that such knowledge initiates a compelling sense of responsibility for discovering a hidden truth. I knew at an intuitive level that I was dissatisfied with my practice and changed it based on an intuitive 'feeling' that I had not articulated. I could now finally move on and ask myself: Why do I do what I do? Why am I concerned about the way I use technology in teaching and learning? Why is it important to me? What is different about what I do and what the teacher in the neighbouring school does? I reflected deeply on these questions. I kept a reflective diary and sought patterns and problems in my account. I read widely around the ideas. I was lucky to be part of a research programme and so had access to good library facilities. I also sought critique and discussed the issues with my teaching colleagues, research colleagues, tutor and critical friends. Even if the ideas were only barely formed in my mind, I was able to share them and invite comment and critique.

And so I did eventually begin to work it out. I gradually saw that my new work practice was the manifestation of my once tacit, but now clarified, ontological and epistemological values around holism in education. I had taken the first step towards aligning my educational values with my practice at an intuitive level. I gradually came to realise that I was taking steps towards working in the direction of my values of love and care for the interconnectedness of people and their environment. I realised that I had intuitively been battling against the isolated and fragmented nature of many educational practices. I came to see that I believed that making connections between various aspects of my educational life was extremely important to me. I drew on the work of Miller (1996, 2007) and Palmer (1993, 1998) and sought to make learning more meaningful by establishing connections between life outside the classroom and life inside, between my students and myself, between school and families and the wider community, between school and the global community, between the word of nature and learning, between children and adults, and so on.

Frequently, the process of identifying an area of professional concern and looking to one's educational values, demonstrated through one's ontological and epistemological commitments, is the first stage of an action research process. The taking of an action or a change in practice often follows. In my case, it was the intuitive change in my practice that gave rise to my interest and concern. I was only able to articulate my understanding of the change in my work when I engaged in deep reflection on my work and came to realise what my educational values were. I was then able to draw on my values as a kind of lens through which I could evaluate my work practices. You may experience the articulation of your educational values in yet a different manner. McIntosh explains: 'Action research in broad terms concerns the lived experiences of people and the understanding of the essences of reality' (2010: 53). Becoming involved in action research is a unique experience for each classroom researcher.

Reflection

When I first set out to examine my practice, I found it very difficult to articulate my understanding of my work. However, I found that partaking in reflective practice and keeping a reflective journal helped me learn more about my work, articulate my concerns about my work and understand why I was concerned. Schön (1995) talks about the uncertainties practitioners experience in their work and explains how, through reflection, a practitioner can make sense of the uncertainties they may allow themselves to experience. I have found that it is a good idea to keep a reflective journal by your side at all times to enable you to record events and your reflections on them, almost as they occur. It is a good idea to jot down these reflections whenever you get a brief moment during the day. Frequently, reflection-in-action (Schön 1983) occurs in your mind as you respond to events in your practice. These may be fleeting thoughts but often they can inform your thinking about your work when you get an opportunity to reflect more deeply. You can then revisit these jottings in a more tranquil frame of mind after work and try to reflect on them and perhaps rewrite them more coherently.

According to Schön, we need to 'observe ourselves in the doing, reflect on what we observe, describe it and reflect on our descriptions' (1995: 30). The act of observing oneself can be difficult because of the busy nature of classrooms. A scribbled thought might be all one can manage in the midst of a busy day. Even if this is the case, it is worth doing because it will help bring the event or thought to life when you revisit it later. It might be possible to have a colleague sit in your classroom on occasion and make observations that might be helpful to your reflective process. The use of video and sound recordings of your work could also be helpful in the reflection process. Appropriate permissions, according to the ethics guidelines of your place of work, must be sought before using them – especially when you are working with children.

Frequently reflective practitioners like to organise their thoughts in specific frameworks such as Schön advises above: they observe, reflect, describe and reflect again. Some reflective practitioners use the day's hastily scribbled notes and make a list of the events on one side of a page and their response and reflections on the other side. Woodward describes this framework as a 'double entry journal' (1998: 417) and emphasises how important it is for each entry to conclude with a section indicating the subsequent proposed action the practitioner wishes take. Loughran (2002) also talks about the importance of reflection with a view towards improving practice. The idea of reflecting on your work with the aim of developing a better understanding of it, taking action towards improving it, and developing a theory from it is key not only to the reflective process but also to the process of action research. Moon (2004: 102) explains how frameworks for reflective writing that incorporate depth of reflection have been developed. She also draws on the work of Hatton and Smith (1995) and describes a model of reflection at four levels: descriptive writing, descriptive reflection, dialogic reflection and critical reflection (2004: 100). While description on its own is considered the least effective level of reflection, Moon explains that some description is always required to give the necessary background details for the reflection; the fourth level of the framework – critical reflection – shows an awareness of a myriad of perspectives and multitudinous historical and social contexts.

Critical thinking

It is important, therefore, that the reflections in your journal are meaningful. Marcos, Sánchez and Tillema (2008) are critical of the quality of reflection found in some reflective accounts. They looked at the published reflective journals of 49 teachers, and found that many of them lacked high level critical engagement with the issues. They suggested that many reflective journals do not record the cyclical nature of reflection–action and that many journal entries solely stress positive outcomes to the solutions provided without engaging with the problems and messiness of real practice. The authors were critical of reflective journals that deal solely with providing solutions to mundane classroom situations without adequate critical engagement.

When you begin to engage in reflective practice and write up a reflective journal, it is important to choose a format that suits your own learning strengths and professional needs. Sometimes, at the outset, it can be interesting to allow your journal to take shape in a free and fairly unstructured way for some days. As you progress, the format that suits you best will emerge. The role of description and of the narrative of your practice is important as you reflect on your practice and try to make meaning of your work. Problematising your practice is also important. Bearing in mind the warnings of Marcos, Sánchez and Tillema (2008), you should consider the importance of critical thinking in your journaling. Try to question the everyday mundane practices in which you engage. Ask yourself 'Why do I do this?' Taylor and White talk about 'reflexivity' as deep and critical reflection: 'Reflexivity suggests that we interrogate these previously taken-for-granted assumptions' (2000: 198). I have found myself that using description solely to outline an event gives rise to unclear and often unsuitable action plans. When you have recorded the event in your journal or told the story, you need to ask yourself why this event is of interest to you. Digging underneath the issues and thinking critically can help to elucidate your thinking and help you make better decisions, which can lead towards committed informed action. Carr and Kemmis (1986) call this *praxis*, and I will discuss this below.

Reflective activity

Ask yourself how you might avoid engaging in practices in an unquestioning and uncritical manner. Look carefully at an entry in your reflective journal and question how your reflection interrogates some taken-for-granted assumptions. How can you improve this, if necessary?

Praxis

According to Carr and Kemmis, praxis is 'informed action which, by reflection on its character and consequences, reflexively changes the "knowledge-base" which informs it . . . praxis is "doing-action" . . . it remakes the conditions of informed action and constantly reviews action and the knowledge which informs it' (1986: 33). As a self-study action researcher I see praxis as an action that is taken as a result of reflection. The action is then reflected upon and this reflection then influences the original thinking that informed the action so that future actions may be altered accordingly. Further action may be modified in light of the new thinking. In praxis, 'Thought and action (or theory and practice), are dialectically related. They are . . . in a process of interaction, which is a continual reconstruction of thought and action' (Carr and Kemmis, 1986: 34). Many action researchers like to insert the word 'critically' before 'informed' to imply that critical engagement with the issues has taken place alongside a commitment to an improved form of practice or praxis (see for example the News South Wales Curriculum and Learning Innovation Centres website at <http://www.curriculumsupport.education.nsw.gov.au/>). So as you begin work on your reflective journal, it is important to remember that the practice in which you engage as a result of this reflection and critical thought may change. It is important to remember also that this process is going to be the basis for your emergent theory, which will be drawn from your practice.

Emerging patterns

You may find that particular patterns, flashpoints or other important issues emerge for you as your journal grows. Zeichner and Liston remind us that reflection 'emancipates us from merely impulsive and routine activity . . . [and] enables us to direct the actions with foresight and to plan according to ends in view of purposes of which we are aware' (1996: 17). As you reflect and think critically about your work, you may find that you begin to approach your work with 'fresh' eyes and that you develop a new enthusiasm around your work. You may find that specific themes, focal points and concerns reoccur throughout your reflection. These are the issues that probably cause you most concern and they may emerge as the focus of your research.

If, in the initial stages of your research, you are unsure about what your educational values are (as I was), undertaking to keep a reflective journal might help you to discover them. The themes or issues that reoccur may help you clarify your values. If you know what your educational values are, then your journal can help you see if you are actually working in the direction of these values, as discussed in Chapters 1 and 2. Remember also that in engaging in self-study action research, you are reflecting on yourself and your practice. Whitehead (1989) reminds us that 'I' am the focus of the research; you are hoping to improve your understanding of your work, or your work practices.

When you get the rhythm of the reflective journal established, it is important to remember that you may not speedily solve the problems that are concerning you. However, you will gain insight into your work and develop a new awareness of how you are working and engaging with others. Schön reminds his readers that the 'proper test of a round of inquiry is not only "Have I solved this problem?" but "Do I like the new problems I have created?"' (1995: 31).

Reflective activity

Ask yourself:

- Why do I do what I do?
- I have identified my area of professional concern and interest; why is this area important to me?
- I would like to change my practice in [name a specific area] because [give a reason].
- I would like to develop my understanding of [name a specific practice] because [give a reason].
- I think that [name a relevant educational issue] is unfair because [give a reason].

Entering into dialogue and seeking critique

One of the key aspects of self-study action research is that you share your thinking with one or more colleagues from the outset and invite critique. In more traditional forms of research, the researcher shares their findings at the end of the research. However, as an action researcher you will find it helpful to share your emergent thoughts with sympathetic colleagues from the outset. This is especially fruitful if you are part of a group of students who meet regularly academically or professionally as part of a post graduate programme. It is important to remember that when people are forming new ideas in their minds, these ideas are not as yet fully formed and therefore should be treated with gentleness and respect. I am drawing here on the thinking of Bohm (2004) as he talks about dialogue as the flow of understanding that emerges between and through people. He describes how new understanding may emerge that was not present at the outset of the dialogue and that such emergent processes are creative and crucial to creating shared meanings between people. If you are studying alone, you might like to ask some work colleagues to be your critical friends.

It is also important to encourage your colleagues to question your thinking and be prepared to disagree respectfully with you. Invite your colleague(s) to ask critical questions like 'Why is this aspect of your work worthwhile?' Explain to your colleagues that discussing ideas that are contrary to your own will help you think more clearly. Colleagues who pretend to agree with you on the false basis of 'friendship' or the fear of hurting your feelings will mislead you. Hargreaves (1994) is critical of this notion of 'contrived collegiality' because it is superficial and wasteful of energy and effort. Critical friends need to be honest with you. Woolly or inconsistent thinking should be challenged – in a respectful manner. You need to prepare yourself, too, for tough criticism and probing questions. Remind yourself that dialogue that dislodges your own fixed ideas and causes you to question your thinking may frequently move your thinking on. The idea is to clarify your thinking and firm up your ideas. Your aim is to engage in meaningful and purposeful research; to achieve this aim, you must have some clear thoughts and well-substantiated arguments.

Sometimes getting time to meet with critical friends can be difficult, especially if they live some distance away from you. Talking over the phone can help alleviate this problem. The use of technology such as e-mail, chat forums, wikis, Skype and Google Docs with colleagues can also extend critical conversations and learning in a meaningful and reflective manner. You might like to sign up to JISCMail's e-forum for beginning action researchers at <https://<http://www.jiscmail.ac.uk/cgi-bin/webadmin?SUBED1=inclusivegandt&A=1&D=0&H=0&O=T&T=0>. Whether you choose to engage in dialogue with one or a number of colleagues, either face to face or through the use of technology, is not overly significant. What is important is that you engage with others and share you thinking with them.

Reflective activity

Ask yourself:

- How can I locate some friends or colleagues with whom I can discuss my emergent ideas?
- How might I ensure that my critical friends will be respectful of me in the vulnerability of my newly formed thinking?
- How can I encourage them to disagree with me and question me if I am not making sense and need some guidance?

Putting 'I' at the heart of your work

As I gradually began to develop an understanding of the underpinning reasons for my concerns, I began to realise that my work was an expression of my desire to establish a more holistic approach to teaching and learning for my class. Miller's thinking is helpful as he suggests that education should be about helping students develop a capacity for connectedness and that if education can be aligned with the interconnectedness and dynamism of nature, then 'the possibilities for fulfilment increase greatly' (2007: 3).

As I peeled back the layers of fixed ideas and complacent thinking in my own mind, I began to understand why I chose to work with technology and why holism was important to me. I developed an emergent understanding of the dissonance I experienced between the external world of filling in workbooks and completing textbooks (Riel 1999) and my new insights into how my values around love and the nurturing of holistic approaches to education (Miller 2007). I had begun to see that technology enabled students to make connections with other people outside of the classroom and the idea of connection was important to me as it was embedded in my educational values around holism. The students used technology to record events where they made connections and carried out projects with the local community, on the local environment and with others in far flung regions of the world. It gave students whose reading and writing skills were weak an opportunity to present work of an equal standard to the other children. All these innovations in my work were an expression of my desire to live in the direction of my values around holism, caring relationships and interconnectedness in education.

When I reflect on the insights I gained here, I realise that at some stage the focus of my attention had changed from myself and how I worked with my pupils to the technology itself. Moon reminds us that 'Depth of reflection seems particularly to be characterized by increased flexibility and ability to manage the framing process in an open and flexible manner' (2004: 102). When I refocused and brought my attention to how I was working and engaging with others I began to gain some clarity in my thinking.

Jack Whitehead has written extensively on the importance of the 'living I' (2000, 2003, 2004, 2007). He says 'I am advocating the inclusion of "I" as an individual who is living relationally in cosmic, global and social spaces' (2007: 1). In advocating the inclusion of 'I' as the focus of self-study action research, Whitehead's thinking is based on the idea that you, the researcher, are the focus of your research. When you undertake self-study action research, you can take responsibility for sustaining and improving yourself and the world you are in (McNiff and Whitehead 2009). I cannot change other people or my students and colleagues; you can only change yourself. You may try to create a productive learning environment for your students; you may hope to influence others positively in the course of your reflection and action, but the focus of your work as an action researcher is on you.

As a self-study action researcher, I examine my practice in a critical and ethical manner. I hope to gain insight into my work or improve my practice so that not only will the quality of my educational life improve, the lives of others will improve also. Wilcox, Watson and Patterson explain the process thus: 'self-study is vital to professional practice. Self-study allows practitioners to engage in inquiry that contributes to their own capacity for expert and caring professional practice while also contributing to the growth of their profession' (2004: 307). When I am the focus of my research, I am clear that this research is about my interactions, responses, attitudes, relationships and responsibilities to others.

Traditionally action researchers used to have to defend the idea of putting 'I' at the centre of the research. In the past, much research in education was written in the third person: using the voice of an external researcher, writing about 'the author' and researching on 'subjects' – the students and teachers in the classroom (Pithouse, Mitchell and Weber 2009). Much of this has now changed in light of the burgeoning interest in self-study and action research. Teachers are now seen as legitimate researchers in their classrooms (Stenhouse 1975), and McNiff (2005) takes Stenhouse's (1975) idea of 'teacher as researcher' further and promotes the idea of the practitioner as theorist (McNiff 2002) and teacher as theorist (McNiff 2005).

As you undertake your action research process, you will use established theories in the literature to inform your thinking about your practice. You may decide to change aspects of your practice in light of your engagement with the literature. Gradually, as you begin to theorise your practice, you will find that the practice in which you engage, and the learning you derive from that, will inform your emergent theory (see Chapter 8). There is an interaction between theory and practice where theory will inform the practice and your practice, in turn, will inform theory. Undertaking action research into one's own work can lead to a greater sense of autonomy and many find it an empowering and liberating process.

New awareness

Sometimes our work in our classrooms is of a repetitive and routine nature. Sometimes the responses we give to our students are also of an unthinking, mechanical nature. You may find as you engage with a self-study action research programme and reflect critically on your work that you are developing a keener sense of awareness of yourself and your thoughts as well as the relationships you have with colleagues and students. You may broaden your awareness of what is happening in your class, and develop a keener sense of the atmosphere in your workplace. You may feel as though you are seeing your workplace and your relationship with others there in a new light. This stepping back from yourself and taking a breather can be inspirational. Don't forget that inspiration literally means 'breathing in'.

This heightened awareness can be helpful as you try to gain insight into your practice and seek to improve it. It may also lead to a more respectful and caring work environment. Yoshida says:

> In modern education, we have forgotten to perceive the child as a whole. We analyse the body, feelings and intelligence, and tend to think that each segment can be developed separately. We need instead to develop an awareness to 'experience the child as a whole, the wholeness of the child'.
>
> (Yoshida 2002: 133)

Noddings (1992) talks about the importance of developing empathy with others, of trying to see life through the eyes of others (especially our students). Moon (2004) explains how depth of reflection can be demonstrated in the researcher's ability to frame emotional factors. So, in developing a keener awareness of your own needs, strengths and difficulties as well as those of the students or colleagues with whom you work, the benefits for all may be manifold.

Reflective activity

Ask yourself:

- How do I develop a keener awareness of my own needs, strengths and difficulties?
- How do I develop a keener awareness of the needs, strengths and difficulties of my colleagues and students?
- How do I demonstrate that I give them ample opportunities to speak?
- How can I show that I listen carefully and respectfully?
- How do I demonstrate that I treat everyone fairly?
- How could I create a calmer, more caring environment in my classroom?
- How can I perceive if there is a particular aspect of my everyday work that might close down the learning process for someone?

Reading

It was important for me to read widely around and think critically about my areas of interest which initial pertained to the inclusion of digital technology in education. I broadened my focus to explore topics such as holism and spirituality in education. I also learned to think critically about these ideas. So, even though I was researching my practice and my understanding of my practice, I was also learning to ask questions about the role of power and equality in my work. In the next chapter I will explore ideas around critical pedagogy in more detail.

I was also drawn to other literatures that seemed initially to be outside my own area of interest. For example, my reading about digital learning led me to literature about the importance of creativity in education (Craft, Jeffrey and Liebling 2001), the quality of care in teaching (Noddings 2005) and literature about love and spirituality (hooks 2003; Palmer 2007). While none of these writings seem to have a direct link with technology, it was through this process of exploring a wider body of literature that I learned to develop an understanding of my own work with digital learning. In my work, I learned through engagement with the literature that my interest in technology had more to do with my desire to develop holistic connections in my work than to do with technology itself.

While it is very important to read widely around your topic of interest and inform your thinking about your practice and related issues, it is also important to feel that you may disagree with what authors say. Very often students, even at postgraduate level, feel they must agree with what the experts say. However, if you disagree with what you read, you must acknowledge that and substantiate your disagreement with a good, robust, counter argument. You will need to read in depth to substantiate your arguments. Reading widely around your topic can often unearth contradictory views to your own, which can sometimes clarify your ideas and help sharpen your thinking. The process of dislodging your convictions can help change your current thinking. As you read, be flexible and prepared to change, and keep an open mind to the thoughts of others, especially those with whom you disagree.

Disagreeing with 'experts' can prove to be difficult. Chomsky warns us that 'once you are educated, you have already been socialized in ways that support the power structure' (2004: 3), and your ability to think critically about the education system and other systems has already been modified unbeknownst to you. Chomsky (2004) is critical of educators who have already subscribed to a non-critical form of thinking. When I set out to research my practice, I read Chomsky's ideas and felt pity for those poor educators who were unable to think critically and who were unaware that they were unable to think critically. It took me some time and a lot of reading and discussion with others to realise that I was actually one of those 'poor' educators myself!

Generally, the marking boards for postgraduate programmes seek active and critical engagement with the literature, so now is the time to begin to engage at a critical level with the literature. At the beginning of your research, you will need to read widely around your topic to inform your thinking. As time goes on, your reading may become more focused. As your ideas become clarified in the research process, you will use the literature to support your arguments and substantiate your emergent theory. If you are affiliated to a college, your course leaders will advise you on how to access journals and locate books that might help you in your learning process. If you are working on your own, it might be helpful to subscribe to an academic journal in your field of interest. Online bookshops often sell second-hand books at a good price and even your local librarian can locate relevant books for you. You could try sending an email to your favourite author; if you are lucky she or he might reply.

It is important also to keep abreast of current thinking around practitioner research. Books like this one are important to help you gain insight into the key aspects of practitioner research. The websites of Jack Whitehead (<http://www.actionresearch.net>) and Jean McNiff (<http://www.jeanmcniff.com>) are also good resources, as is the journal *Educational Action Research*, for example.

It is a good idea to keep notes of the key points of interest in any book or article you read. When you revisit it in six months time, you will remember it much more easily if you have made an *aide mémoire* with some reminders of the key points.

Reflective activity

Ask yourself:

- Where can I locate some books or journals directly connected to my area of interest?
- How can I identify a wider source of reading that is not directly linked to my topic but might broaden my thinking?
- How can I locate some books, journals or reputable websites that will help my understanding of action research?

Summary

You have already seen in Chapters 1 and 2 how you might identify an area of special interest to you in your practice. In this chapter you examined some ideas around Whitehead's (2007) question 'Why am I concerned?' and examined some strategies that could be used to help you gain a better understanding of your practice. You discovered that a self-study action research approach is not necessarily a neat linear process. You are involved in a complex research process and how it progresses is as individual and unique as you and your thinking. However, if you are serious about trying to improve your practice or your understanding of your practice, and to generate a theory from your practice, it is important to query the 'givens' of your everyday practices and to think critically about what you do and why.

To assist you in the process, it is helpful to begin a meaningful reflective diary, where you question your stories and examine your ideas in a critical manner. It is also very important to read widely and critically around your area of interest, to read broadly around related topics, and to keep up to date on current thinking in the field of research. You need to remember, also, that 'I' am the focus of the research. You are researching yourself, your thinking and your work practices. However, you are also balancing the needs of others, your students, colleagues or other people, along with that all important 'I'.

As your theory begins to emerge, it is prudent to share your ideas with colleagues, in a safe and respectful space, and enter into critical and supportive dialogue. Sharing the half-formed ideas that emerge as you aim to improve your practice will help clarify your thinking for you.

In the next chapter I will develop these ideas further and help you locate your concerns and questions in the wider canvas of critical pedagogy and contradiction.

Further reading

Carr, W. and Kemmis, S. (1986) *Becoming Critical: Education, Knowledge and Action Research*, London: Falmer Press.
    An ideal book to awaken or reawaken critical thinking for educators.
Clandinin, D.J., Downey, C.A. and Huber, J. (2009) 'Attending to Changing Landscapes: Shaping the Interwoven Identities of Teachers and Teacher Educators', *South Pacific Journal of Teacher Education*, 37(2), 141–54.
    Looks at teachers' narratives and explores the educational landscape.
Dadds, M. and Hart, S. (2001) *Doing Practitioner Research Differently*, London: RoutledgeFalmer.
    A great introduction to thinking outside the traditional forms of research and doing research a little differently.
McIntosh, P. (2010) *Action Research and Reflective Practice: Creative and Visual Methods to Facilitate Reflection and Learning*. London: Routledge.
    An exhortation to move away from mechanical approaches to action research and reflective practice, and to look at more creative approaches.
McNiff, J. (2002) *Action Research for Professional Development: Concise Advice for New Action Researchers*, 3rd edn, available online at <http://www.jeanmcniff.com/ar-booklet.asp> (accessed 25 May 2011).
    This is a freely downloadable document outlining some of the basic ideas for new action researchers.
McNiff, J. and Whitehead, J. (2010) *You and Your Action Research Project*, 3rd edn, London: RoutledgeFalmer.
    This is a very helpful text to get your research started and gives some good guidelines for writing up research.
Mellor, N. (2001) 'Messy Method: The Unfolding Story', *Educational Action Research*, 9(3), 465–84.
    An excellent paper for researchers who are getting caught up in the messiness of the research.

Moon, J. (2004) *A Handbook of Reflective and Experiential Learning: Theory and Practice*, London: RoutledgeFalmer.

Palmer, P.J. (1998) *The Courage to Teach: Exploring the Inner Landscape of a Teacher's Landscape*, San Francisco: Jossey-Bass.

An inspirational book, which is very suitable for educators who are trying to reconnect with why they became involved in education in the first place.

Pithouse, K., Mitchell, C. and Weber, S. (2009) 'Self-study in Teaching and Teacher Development: A Call to Action', *Educational Action Research*, 17(1), 43–62.

A motivational paper that reminds classroom researchers of the importance of their work.

Schön, D. (1983) *The Reflective Practitioner: How Professionals Think in Action*, New York: Basic Books.

A classic book on the importance of reflective practice.

Chapter 4

Thinking critically about educational practices

This chapter explores ideas around:

- epistemology
- how one might experience oneself as a living contradiction (White-head 1989)
- how critical pedagogy can be important in our everyday lives
- looking at a model for working through the question 'Why am I interested?'

Introduction

In this chapter I will develop ideas around discovering why you might be interested in particular aspects of your work. Articulating the reasons for your concerns will give you a good foundation for your research as you work towards improving your practice and generating a theory from that practice. I will outline Whitehead's thinking (1989) around 'experiencing oneself as a living contradiction' and explain how it can be a cornerstone of an action research process. I will explore the inner conflict that may arise for practitioners as they see inconsistencies between their own educational values and their daily work practices. I will explain how some issues that arise for educators have a more political and systemic nature. Some ideas of critical pedagogy are examined and located in the everyday practices of the educator.

In the latter part of the chapter, you will be guided through a practical exercise. Here you will be encouraged to engage in critical thinking about your practice and draw up a brief outline of why you are concerned about your practice and how you might best understand it. This final section may also serve as a guide for you if you wish to write up your own research report.

Value-laden practice

As an educator, you probably hold some educational values. As you have read in Chapters 1 and 2, these values help inform how you, as a teacher, do your everyday work. They guide you in the relationships you have with your students and colleagues. They help you decide on the particular methodologies and teaching strategies you might choose. They also help you to respond appropriately in challenging situations. However, sometimes when practitioners reflect on their work, they see that aspects of it or their attitudes to it are in conflict with those values that guide how they think about and live their professional lives.

Many educationalists challenge the idea of education as a neutral concept. For example, Whitehead talks about education being a value-laden practice (1989). He describes values as being embodied in practice and explains that their meaning can be articulated throughout one's practice. Using Whitehead's ideas, you can see how if you value respect, for example, you try to act in a respectful manner towards yourself, your colleagues and your students. Educational values are informed by ontological and epistemological values. By ontological I mean the values I hold around my being; how I am in the world and how I am with others. When I think about my epistemological values, I think about how I see knowledge, how it is generated, what counts as knowledge and who decides. When I reflected on my practice, I perceived that my ontological and epistemological values around care and connection were being denied in some aspects of my practice, and this caused me concern. We have already explored some ideas around ontological values in Chapters 1 and 2. Now I will look at some ideas around epistemological values.

Looking at my epistemological stance

When I think about issues to do with knowledge and how knowledge is generated, I can see that my epistemological stance has changed over the years and therefore so too have my epistemological values. This has wide-ranging implications because not only does my epistemological stance inform how I teach and shape the kind of relationship I have with my students, it also informs the methodology I choose for my research.

Some years ago, I saw my role as a teacher as that of one who transmitted a commodity called knowledge (Apple 2004; Ball 2004; Brown 2002). I was an agent finishing textbooks and filling in workbooks; fulfilling the intentions of what I understood to be curriculum. I now realise that instead of engaging with the curriculum in a meaningful manner, I was focused on completing workbooks. I equated finishing a textbook with doing a good job. I saw knowledge as a deliverable package, something that could be bestowed upon people. Let us think for a minute about the act of *bestowing* something, and about the power relations and ideas around knowledge that are embedded in that act. The person who bestows often holds the privilege and possibly the power, whereas the recipient is frequently more or less powerless. Sometimes there is an expectation that the recipient ought to be indebted and grateful for the bestowal.

The idea of the power-constituted nature of knowledge-based relationships draws on Foucault's (1980a) thinking that locates power in the capillary-like actions within the relationships that people have with one another. Traditional perceptions of the student as a passive recipient have been critiqued by social constructivists such as Vygotsky (1978) and researched by Devine (2003), among others. Issues of power and knowledge are frequently interlinked and as you think about your epistemological stance, it is good to develop an awareness of this connection. The notion that knowledge is solely something that can be packaged and given to someone is also open to question. However, as I reflect on my epistemological stance of some years ago, I can see that I held my beliefs in an unquestioning manner and I saw that 'knowledge is a gift bestowed by those who consider themselves knowledgeable upon those whom they consider to know nothing' (Freire 2003: 58). It is interesting to note that this epistemological stance continues to be held in many educational settings today.

Now I think differently. I have come to see that I now understand knowledge and knowledge generation as being something quite different; not just as a commodity (although it can be) that can be passed on but more as a process that is fluid, organic and emergent; something that can be generated or created. I like Bohm's (2004) description of dialogical ways of knowing as a 'stream of meaning' that flows through people such that a new understanding may emerge. I have seen my own role shifting from being a teacher who is solely a transmitter of factual knowledge (although frequently I must do this too) to that of one who is developing an awareness of the wholeness and individuality of my students while nurturing their strengths and addressing their needs. I have tried to embody an epistemology of wholeness, interconnectedness and context, as suggested by Miller (2007) as I work with my class. This change in my epistemological stance produced a different type of dynamic in my classroom, one that perceived the student as a valid knower and teacher in their own right. Freire describes this well: 'The teacher is no longer merely the-one-who teaches, but one who is himself [sic] taught in dialogue with the students, who in turn while being taught also teach. They become responsible for a process in which all grow' (2003: 63).

This shift in my thinking has also enabled me to become an action researcher (or perhaps becoming an action researcher enabled me to change my epistemological stance, I am not sure). Remember, your ontological and epistemological assumptions influence your methodological choice for your research (see Cohen, Manion and Morrison 2007). If I see knowledge and knowledge generation as something external to myself, then my research approach would have to be from an externalist's perspective. However, I see myself as someone who interacts with others, who comes to know through dialogue with others and whose educational values illuminate how I work; therefore I am drawn to an action research methodology. In truth, I am drawn to an action research way of life.

Reflective activity

Ask yourself how you perceive knowledge and knowledge generation.

Experiencing oneself as a living contradiction

Jack Whitehead (see Whitehead and McNiff 2006) has written extensively around the idea of 'experiencing oneself as a living contradiction'. While this may sound as though this is a complex concept, in its most basic form, it is a concept many people meet daily. It occurs when you do not live according to the values you hold. For example, if a person values having an organised office space but in fact they just have piles of letters and manuals stacked untidily everywhere, they might experience themselves as a living contradiction. There exists a divergence between what the person holds as a value for themselves and how they actually live or practice their daily work.

Whitehead and McNiff (2006) also suggest that the space in which one experiences oneself as a living contradiction can provide the researcher with a good starting point for their research. They may ask questions like 'How can I improve my practice?', 'How can I improve my understanding of my work?' or 'Why do I need to focus on this aspect of my practice?' It can be a place of conflict between what an educator might want for themselves and their students and the reality of the education system of which they are part.

Carr and Kemmis (1986: 84) differentiate between contradiction and paradox. They say that when people speak about contradiction, there is an inherent understanding that a solution or compromise may be reached. However, when people speak about paradox, an incompatibility between the two ideas is assumed. As action researchers, it is important to remember that we are working with contradiction and are aiming to diminish the differences between our values and our practice – should they exist; we are at least seeking a compromise and at best a good match.

Sometimes, when novice researchers begin to reflect on their values and see how there might be a discrepancy between their values and how they work in their everyday practice, they become discouraged when they see how they 'fail' to live in the direction of their values. However, how one experiences oneself as a living contradiction need not be a negative experience. It can be – and usually is – an opportunity for growth and learning. It is important to remember that we are merely human and by this admission we need to acknowledge our own imperfections and frailties. Berlin cites Kant's words 'Out of the crooked timber of humanity no straight thing was ever made' (1990: 19) to remind people that humanity by its nature is imperfect and flawed. Sometimes these imperfections and flaws are what add colour, interest and nuance to how we live, as well as make our lives interesting. They are most certainly instrumental in assisting us to live in ways that are contrary to the values we hold.

Whitehead describes his own ideas thus:

> individuals experience themselves as living contradictions in the sense that they experience a tension of holding together the values that constitute their humanity and the experience of their denial in practice. This stimulates their

imagination on action plans that are intended to enable the values to be lived more fully in practice.

(Whitehead 2005: 4)

This tension is key not just to action research but also to what I see as being human. It encapsulates our free will to choose and our capacity to think for ourselves. It reminds us of our imperfections and failings because as humans we are not pre-programmed robots who can exhibit behaviours and work practices exactly as is expected of us. Being human means that sometimes we make choices that are unwise and sometimes we make mistakes. We hold specific values and beliefs that frequently inform us how we should live our lives, and yet sometimes we act in direct opposition to them. Sometimes, when practitioners unearth discrepancies between their values and how they live them in their practice, they can become disillusioned by this perceived failure. Sometimes, such insights can cause practitioners to wallow in self-doubt. However, looking at how one might be experiencing oneself as a living contradiction should not result in a dead-end of recrimination or feeling guilty because this could lead to a lack of growth in our thinking processes. Instead, it is more productive to choose instead to 'forgive and remember' as Shulman (2002) suggests, and to use our 'mistakes' or personal experiences as living contradictions as a spring board for improving our practices. Experiencing oneself as a living contradiction should be grounds for celebration and renewed learning. It is a very invigorating and productive concept to perceive that a place of human frailty can bring about new creativity and possibly facilitate the emergence of ground-breaking theory. This is what we, the authors of this book, hope to tap into as we work through some ideas around action research. The following is a short example from my own experience.

Experiencing myself as a living contradiction

As I learned to experience myself as a living contradiction (Whitehead 1989), I began to see that the educational values I held around care and the recognition of the human nature of people were not enacted in my everyday work. There was an imbalance between my values and the everyday expectations of the education system. I had developed a sense of unease around, what I liked to call the 'finish-the-textbook' approach to education; the approach I had used for over 20 years of my teaching life. I had learned to equate good teaching with the completion of textbooks and workbooks.

As I began to become more comfortable with my role as teacher, I developed a niggling sense of uncertainty around the usefulness of 'finish-the-textbook' and rote-learning approaches to education (Freire 1970). Unconsciously I had begun to develop projects for my class that involved communications with other classes using multimedia and digital technology in the form of web pages and e-mail communications. I had started to involve people from outside the school in my work and I began to explore the local natural environment as a regular part of my schoolwork. These new approaches to teaching and learning for me were indicative of my first tentative steps towards bridging the gaps between my values around holism in education and my practice.

In the above vignette, it is clear that I had not yet begun to think critically or be able to answer questions like 'Why do I practice in this manner?' However, at a tacit level (Polanyi 1958), I had begun to develop practices that were more commensurate with my educational values, without even being able to articulate what those values were for a long time. For many, the examination of one's ontological and epistemological values happens before any change in practice occurs or any action is taken. In either scenario, it is important to develop an awareness of how you might experience yourself as a living contradiction.

In the action research process, the identification of areas where you might be experiencing yourself as a living contradiction can often provide you with the launch pad to improving your practice or developing a better understanding of your work. It was imperative to critical thinkers like Freire that educators acknowledge that 'oppression does not exist within a closed world from which there is no exit' and instead that they 'embrace fully this dialectical understanding of our relationship with the world and transform our teaching into . . . revolutionary praxis' (Darder, Baltodano and Torres 2003: 54). When you engage in an action research process, you embrace the idea that once you experience yourself as a living contradiction you can then transform your teaching. Chapters 5 to 8 will help you lay out a plan of action towards improvement and developing a theory of practice from that process.

Reflective activity

Ask yourself:

- What educational values can I connect with my ontological and epistemological beliefs?
- What are the areas in my everyday practices that are not in keeping with my values?
- How might I do something about improving these practices or improving my understanding of them?
- How might my journal writing assist me as I experience myself as a 'living contradiction'?

Reflection–action cycle

Very often, your first exploration of a reflection–action cycle can result in the unearthing of valuable insights. Teachers often identify an area of relevance for themselves by expressing their dissatisfaction with the teaching methodology they have chosen or the practices in which they frequently engage. You may find that these concerns might include issues like pupils not handing in homework, children making no oral contribution in class, students having bad manners or poor concentration, or teachers having 'teacher's pets' for example.

These are important discoveries for any teacher as they begin to take an action research cycle. The teacher, who has now become a researcher, tries to question themselves around why these issues are significant for them. They look at their practice through the lens of their ontological and epistemological values and find that some times these are the areas in which they are experiencing themselves as a living contradiction. They use their reflective journals to help them gain clarity. They focus on this area and think about ways they can improve their work practices or understanding of their work practices as they prepare a plan of action. Then they take action towards improvement and develop an educational theory from that process. This is one of the defining features of self-study action research. You will see in the following chapters the steps you can take to ameliorate your practice or thinking about your work. As your research unfolds your educational theory, drawn from your practice, will emerge.

As you experience yourself as a living contradiction, you may begin to think about change and improvement. For many, change takes place after serious critical reflection, engagement with literature and educational dialogue with colleagues. In the process of thinking, reflecting, planning, acting and reflecting again, your thinking may change or your mind may open to new ideas or practices. This may enable you to see the world in a new perspective. This new vision and seeing the world anew is a form of new learning in itself. This new learning might highlight how specific methodologies in your practice might need improvement. Your new insight might also inform how you see yourself in relation to others or how you might see knowledge and its generation; it may influence your ontological and epistemological commitments.

When you reach this stage of your research project, where you ask yourself questions like 'Why am I concerned?', 'Why do I do what I do?' or 'Why am I focused on this aspect of my work?', it is important to remember that *you* are at the centre of your research. Your area of interest may pertain to how certain children do not speak out in class, for example, but the focus of your research is you and your engagement with, attitude to, and expectations for these children. If you want to change something in your work for the better, it is important to remember that most sustainable change must start with yourself. Often, research papers in education are written from an external perspective, where the researcher is examining the school or class as an outsider evaluating the situation. In the past, the external perspective was very popular and considered to be the most appropriate for educational research (Pithouse, Mitchell and Weber 2009). While much research is still undertaken from an external perspective, our attention in this book is on self-study action research, which means the focus of the research is you and your connections with others. However, when you read a lot of literature written from an external perspective, it is easy to slip into that external mode of thinking yourself. When you engage in practitioner research you need to remember that you are researching yourself and your thinking, attitudes and relationships with others.

Exploring critical pedagogy

Sometimes when practitioners reflect critically about a specific area of interest in their everyday work and begin to explore their ideas in depth, they find that their concern has less to do with teacher preparation or teaching methodologies and more to do with 'bigger' issues that have origins outside the classroom. Critical pedagogy looks at the issue of power in teaching and learning. It focuses on the politics of education and how and in whose interests knowledge is produced and 'passed on', and views the ideal aims of education as emancipatory. (Burbules and Beck (2009) have written an interesting paper comparing critical thinking and critical pedagogy.) Paolo Freire (2003), the inspirational Brazilian educationalist and exponent of critical pedagogy, never confined his questions about education to methodology or the practical aspects of teaching alone. He believed that issues of power, oppression and culture existed in many aspects of education and he sought to unravel their existence. According to Kemmis (2006), many current action researchers seem to focus on improving teaching techniques without perceiving such techniques as an aspect of the broader issue of the education of people for a better society. Kemmis considers such forms of action research to be inadequate.

I taught a boy called Pat some years ago. He was an affable, pleasant and hard-working student. His ability to locate missing items and remember where people in the class (especially myself) had left specific objects, and his giftedness at making a place tidy and neat was outstanding. His willingness to help and his ability to restore order into a classroom that could be fairly (very) untidy and disorganised was beyond my own capability and understanding. He was unassuming, gentle and genial. Yet, his end-of-year standardised test scores were always low and unimpressive. This was not because Pat was lazy or inattentive. He always did his best but he simply was unable to achieve high scores in tests because his learning strengths were not of a mathematical or linguistic nature.

Despite my best efforts to make the learning process meaningful for Pat, I could never tap into that part of his learning that might have shone some light on maths and language for him. I looked at his school reports over the years and while all his teachers found him to be a great asset to the class and a pleasant and kind boy, his test scores were always low. I found this to be frustrating and wearisome. School reports and test scores were like a summative evaluation of his work for the year and yet they painted a very inaccurate picture of who Pat was. I struggled with the unfairness of this. (These comments are based on my reflective journal, March 2004.)

Let us look at a practical example of how I experienced the insights of critical pedagogy in my own work.

As I reflected on Pat's plight and my sense of frustration, I reread Freire and remembered his advice about the mistake of directing questions around education to methodology or the practical aspects of teaching alone. As Pat's teacher, I needed to make myself more aware that evaluating his worth as a person through standardised test scores was disturbingly unfair and unjust. Sometimes, as educators, we need to step outside ourselves and the education system of which we are part to be able to see more clearly what is happening in our situation. As educators it is sometimes easy to forget that the system can neglect students whose learning strengths are nor linguistic or mathematical, for example, and in this instance I needed to 'step outside' myself to see what was happening more clearly. Pat was part of a system that unfairly values maths and language skills over social skills. Lomax and Whitehead (1996) echo this idea when they speak about oppression being in the minds of people through 'the imposition of values and practices that disable us from participating as fully as we might in our educational enterprises and imposed change that alienates us by appearing to devalue our educational values and practices' (cited in Holley 1997: 2).

I began to see how my concerns about power, oppression and culture pertained not only to political issues but also to everyday matters in my own classroom. The dilemma with Pat was entering into the realm of critical pedagogy and I enjoyed reading the works of Paolo Freire, Maxine Greene, Henry Giroux, bell hooks and Peter McLaren, among others, to help inform my thinking in this area. (You might find it helpful to see a video clip of Henry Giroux being interviewed by Joe Kincheloe at <http://www.freireproject.org/content/henry-giroux-interview>.) Darder describes critical pedagogy thus:

> The fundamental commitment of critical educators is to empower the powerless and transform those conditions which perpetuate human injustice and inequity. . . . Hence, a major function of critical pedagogy is to critique, expose, and challenge the manner in which schools impact upon the political and cultural life of students. Teachers must recognize how schools unite knowledge and power and how through this function they can work to influence or thwart the formation of critically thinking and socially active individuals.
>
> (Darder 1995: 329)

Reflective activity

Ask yourself:

- As I seek to improve my practice or my understanding of my practice, what are the broader issues that are relevant?
- Where in my everyday practice can I locate issues of power, oppression or culture?

Pat was part of an inequitable situation. I came to see that, despite my best efforts, education can be a dispiriting and unjust process for many students. Lynch talks about the tight system of control in education that 'creates great injustices and frustrations for those who cannot find a sense of achievement within it' (Lynch, 1999: 276). I could see how Pat might never find a sense of achievement in the education system. His assessments at most educational institutions would always probably be of a linguistic and mathematical nature and his test scores would always probably be low. Lynch continues, 'different forms of knowledge and relatedly different forms of ability do not have parity of esteem within schools' (1999: 276). Pat's ability to observe keenly and his neatness and generosity of spirit were never going to be acknowledged formally by the education system, but would be highly valued in many workplace settings.

The frustration I experienced around this could not be addressed by the methodologies I employed or the practical aspects of my teaching alone; it was part of a much bigger question to do with power and culture and embedded in critical pedagogy. While the state is obliged to ensure that all children receive an education, I believe that this obligation is frequently only observed at the level of rhetoric. There seems to be an increasing focus on students whose talents lie in linguistic and mathematical areas. The reality for many students is that their needs are not catered for. Students still have to sit state examinations at the end of their schooling at second level to assess their 'ability'. Ultimately the emphasis in the examination is on linguistic and mathematical skills. According to McLaren (2003), standardised tests, with their focus on maths and language skills, are seen as one way of ensuring that schools play their role in improving economic competitiveness. Pat and a large number of other people like him are cast by the wayside as schools become drivers for economic recovery and growth.

While I might be unable to change the unjust focus on the linguistic and mathematical skills in the education system, I am at least aware of them now. Chomsky says that attempts to control the public mind through education systems are not only located within the academy, but begin at an early age

> through a socialization process that is also a form of indoctrination that works against independent thought in favour of obedience. Schools function as a mechanism of this socialization. The goal is to keep people from asking

questions that matter about important issues that directly affect them and others.

(Chomsky 2004: 24)

In my everyday practice I try to give children whose learning strengths lie outside the mathematical and linguistic area an opportunity to learn in a way that might suit their learning needs. In the process of my research, I tried to ask questions that investigated 'important issues'. I tried to bear in mind hooks' observation that 'teachers who are wedded to using the same teaching style every day, who fear any digression from the concrete lesson plan, miss the opportunity for full engagement in the learning process' (2003: 134). I tried neither to fear digression nor to miss opportunities for full engagement in the learning process.

As educators, we know that the reform of institutions takes place slowly and that waiting for the reform of education systems can cause teachers to become tired and cynical (Palmer 2007). Palmer suggests that there is an alternative to waiting. He suggests that people may make a connection with their 'inner reality' and may use this connection to transform their work and their lives. He reminds us that 'we became teachers because we once believed that ideas and insight are at least as real and powerful as the world that surrounds us' (2007: 10) and that teachers need to reconnect with their inner lives of identity and integrity. In the course of my research, I tried to reconnect with an inner reality and to develop a keener awareness of the integrity and identity that brought me to teaching. I used this awareness to illuminate how I taught. I also tried to take opportunities to speak to other educators about the unfairness of our educational system and to draw their attention to how they might engage in critical pedagogy for themselves.

Reflective activity

Ask yourself:

- Why do I feel uncomfortable about how some students are faring in the school system?
- Do I greet all students when I meet them (McLaren 2003)? Why?
- Do I praise academic students more (McLaren 2003) and what does this signify?
- Do I give boys an opportunity to speak more than girls (McLaren 2003)?
- Do I reward middle-class speaking voices (McLaren 2003)? If so, why might this be?
- How might I connect with my own sense of identity and integrity so as to illuminate how I teach?

A model to help explore questions like 'Why am I concerned?'

Now I am going to explore a model, which might help you develop a clearer understanding of your practice and explanations for why you have concerns about or have developed a specific interest in some aspects your work.

There are nine interlinking steps in Figure 4.1. There is no hierarchy in these steps. It is a good idea to take all the steps, but not necessarily in the order in which they are laid out here. You will probably find after some time that each step feeds onto another step and is dependent on at least one other step. They are like interlinking pieces in a jigsaw. After some time, and with a little practice, when you stop to reflect on your work and to ask why you are concerned about it or have an interest in certain aspects of it, you will use all steps more or less together, nearly all the time. You may also find that you need to add more steps into the model to suit your own needs. As you work through the steps for perhaps a second or third time, you may find that your thinking has changed. Changing your thinking in not necessarily an indicator of indecisiveness (though it may be); it is probably more of an indicator that you are learning and your learning is changing your thinking. Having an open mind and being ready for change is part of the organic process of practitioner research.

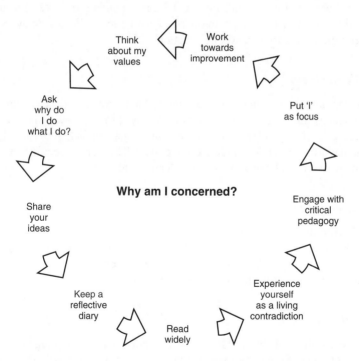

Figure 4.1   Steps towards discovering why I am concerned about a particular area of my work

Towards improvement

As a practitioner researcher, I work towards improvement. I may want to improve my practice or my understanding of my practice, or both. In the course of my research, I will generate new knowledge and theory. I may also influence other educators and create a wider circle of social improvement.

Think about values

I need to be aware of what my ontological and epistemological values are. They may not be immediately apparent to me, but I can gradually allow them to emerge. These values inform how I teach and learn. My everyday work is the enactment of my values. They guide me as I experience myself as a living contradiction. When I do any research, my ontological and epistemological values will inform the methodology I choose for my research.

Why do I do what I do?

As I reflect on my work, I need to think critically about the routine practices I do every day. I ask myself if these practices are worthwhile and if they enhance the learning processes for my students, or if I am depending on taken-for-granted assumptions. I also ask if I am being fair and just in my dealings with everyone. I connect with how I can improve the situation.

Share your ideas

As I undertake this learning process, I am probably going to develop new ideas and change my thinking and understanding. As my learning grows, I need to share my ideas (even if they are not fully formed) and engage in dialogue with others so as to gain clarity and understanding around them. Through respectful but critical dialogue with others, I can allow my new learning to emerge.

Reflective journal

When I write in my reflective journal and reflect on my actions (Schön 1983) I can track issues that arise for me in my work, keep a record of my critical thinking about issues, and make plans for action. Very often the cyclical nature of my reflective journal informs my action research project.

Read widely

As I engage with a wide body of literature, I deepen my understanding of the issues that are significant for me. I also read around more peripheral areas to broaden my thinking. Reading the most current thinking on self-study, reflective practice and living theory can help me to keep abreast of the most current thinking in action research.

Living contradiction

One of the key aspects of action research for me is how I experience myself as a living contradiction (Whitehead 1989). Whenever I try to clarify why I am concerned about particular areas of my work or my understanding of it, I remind myself what my educational values are. I usually find that by looking at the issues that concern me though the lens of my educational values I can find areas where I am not living according to my values; I experience myself as a living contradiction. This not only offers me insights into why I am interested in certain aspects of my practice, but also gives me a launch pad for my research project.

Critical pedagogy

When I reflect on my work and my dissatisfaction with certain aspects of it, especially when I experience myself as a living contradiction, I remind myself of Freire's (2003) warnings not to confine my questions to teaching methodologies or practical issues alone, but also to be aware of issues of power, oppression and culture in many aspects of education.

Making 'I' the focus for the research

While much educational research is written from the perspective of an external researcher, when I am taking a self-study action research approach to my research, I am focusing on myself and how I improve myself in relation to others. When I think about focusing on myself, it is always about me in relation to others. As a teacher, my focus is often on how I can create a more equitable or stimulating learning environment for my class or how I can encourage my class to be more aware of the world of nature around them.

Chapter summary

In this chapter you have examined some ideas around how your epistemological stance (and your ontological beliefs) inform your approach to teaching and learning, and to how you might approach research. You have also explored Whitehead's (1989) ideas around how you might experience yourself as a living contradiction. You have drawn a connection between that experience and developing an insight into why particular areas of your practice might be of concern or interest to you. You have also examined some ideas around why critical pedagogy has an important role in action research. You have explored a nine-step model for helping you work towards discovering why you are concerned about your work. In the next part of the book we will outline what you can do about the issues you have identified by making a plan, carrying it out and collecting data.

Further reading

Chomsky, N. (2004) *Chomsky on Miseducation*, Oxford: Rowman & Littlefield.
Chomsky calls for educational change and is critical of current systems which 'miseducate' students.

Darder, A., Baltodano, M. and Torres, R.D. (eds) (2003) *The Critical Pedagogy Reader*, New York and London: Routledge.
A great collection of essays from the major proponents of critical pedagogy. The book includes a section on how one might put critical theory into practice in the classroom.

Freire, P. (1970) *Pedagogy of the Oppressed*, New York: Seabury.
A classic book and a must-have for anyone exploring critical pedagogy.

hooks, b. (2003) *Teaching Community: A Pedagogy of Hope*, New York: Routledge.
hooks draws some compelling narratives from her own practice to discuss issues such as racism and sexism, and express her joy in teaching.

Noffke, S. and Somekh, B. (2009) *The SAGE Handbook of Educational Action Research*, London: Sage.
A collection of essays from many of the key thinkers in action research. This valuable book highlights the many approaches, methodologies and understandings that are encapsulated in the term 'action research'.

Schmertzing, R. (2007) 'Expert Researchers and School Practitioners: An Historical Perspective on the Marginalization of Practitioner Research and the Silencing of Practitioner Voices', *Journal of Education*, 133(1), 1–24.
A thought-provoking paper discussion the value of the practitioner's voice and the influences of hegemony as that voice is silenced.

Whitehead, J. (2007) 'The Significance of "I" in Living Educational Theories' (draft), available online at <http://www.actionresearch.net/writings/jack/jwchptroutledge150507.htm> (accessed 25 May 2011).
Outlines the importance of locating oneself as the focus of practitioner research.

Part 3

What to do about the questions identified?

Caitriona McDonagh

This part is about developing a personal action plan and gathering data to show any changes or enhancement of your practice. It also investigates the rationale for the research choices you can make. Our decision to place discussion of methodological choices in this part is based on our experiences as teachers and researchers who are both consumers and creators of knowledge. As Kincheloe (2003) suggests, we are advocating conducting meaningful, relevant and rigorous research and, following from this, engaging in the debate around education research.

Chapter 5 discusses information gathering methods to show others what you do when addressing your research topic. Using examples from my classroom research I suggest a five-staged approach to support you in your research. I stress how the values that you have identified in earlier sections have a significant impact on how you conduct your research. Activities are included to help you deal with practical issues such as getting permission from those involved in your research, which is an ethical requirement if you intend to gain accreditation for your research. With such examples I show how you can move from a stance of an activist professional, enquiring into your practice, to a research stance by engaging with the literature and justifying the research methods you choose. Sachs (2003) describes how activist teachers are part of a 'transformative professionalism', which celebrates the balancing of the complexities of teachers' classrooms and identities against the standards of accountability and autonomy.

Chapter 6 is about choosing an overall research approach that is in tune with what you believe is important in education. This involves looking at main research paradigms to confirm if they are appropriate for your work situation and the forms of knowledge that are most valued there. There are examples from my research and exercises to help you document your research in relation to these paradigms. As Kincheloe (2003) suggests, this offers possibilities for teachers and researchers to construct an emancipating system of meaning, exploring assumptions behind education research in order to rediscover professional autonomy and enhance classroom practice so as to improve the quality of education for students.

Chapter 5

How do I show the situation as it is and as it evolves?

This chapter explores:

- suggestions for making a research plan and how to carry it out through a process of action, reflection, learning and evaluation
- information gathering methods and how to get permission from those involved in your research
- the importance of the values you have identified in making decisions about how to conduct your research.

Introduction

Planning and conducting action research in your classroom includes finding ways to document practical changes and changes in your personal perspectives. Previous chapters suggested how you might name an issue that you wish to investigate and critically think about it. During this process you will have noticed that your personal perspectives are not static. What happens in classrooms is not static either. The complexities of teachers' work do not lend themselves to a definitive model for researching one's practice. So, instead of offering a model for classroom research, this chapter offers suggestions on how to adopt a pragmatic approach. Research methods that have real relevance to your work situation are needed because you are not only examining your work in the hope of improving professionally but also looking for ways to make your new ideas public for critical evaluation. As well as being distinctively personal research, I am looking at ways to generate theory *through* action. I am suggesting a classical five-stage approach to action research, but by clarifying the values base of your research and your philosophical stance you can move from action towards theory generation.

This chapter aims to guide you through this process by including my experiences of planning to take action in my classroom to show the situation as it was and as it evolved. There were five stages in which this occurred, which I will use to explain the process and help you work through it:

- I began my classroom research actions by looking at some possibilities to address the issues I was interested in.
- I planned what to do.
- I carried out my plan.
- I evaluated it.
- I examined what followed from what I had done.

Throughout these stages I reflected on the relationships between what I was doing and the values I hold about education.

How to research the issue you are interested in

The first phase of an action research process is to set out some possibilities to show how you might research the issue you are interested in. Possibilities that often spring to teachers' minds are to find literature on the issue that concerns them, including policy documents and curricula, or to use practical approaches that are within their own current repertoire of classroom actions. A frequent research possibility that teachers consider is to test, teach and retest, because it is a very familiar process to us. It is an essential component of a successful teaching and learning process in any classroom or school. Assessment for learning involves the systematic gathering of information to influence the next steps in pupils learning (National Council for Curriculum Assessment 2007). It is also a very practical way to approach a research question, because if you can demonstrate or test the situation, take action and follow up with a re-evaluation of the situation, you have established a basic action research process. This process will have more practical relevance to you when you evaluate it against the ontological and epistemological values that you have already considered in previous chapters. To do this you could ask questions similar to those in earlier chapters, like 'Why are you doing this?', 'What motivates you?' and 'What forms of knowledge inform your decisions?'

These questions are of particular importance when sourcing a suitable assessment tool for your research. The question 'Why are you doing this?' often requires teachers to consider what they plan to do about government policy, curricular demands, school policies and practices, or current theories around teaching and learning. These are frameworks that explain the contexts that influence you in choosing possible actions.

'What motivates you?' is a question about the life values that you hold and how they relate to your plan to investigate the issue of interest to you. So your conceptual framework will include the values you identified in the previous parts of this book. For example, in my research I was looking at ideas around equity, democracy and freedom, and focusing on ability rather than disability. Each of these frames brought its own specific literature. Engaging with a wide variety of literatures is time-consuming but many teacher-researchers do not find that this additional reading is a burden because of their passion for the issues they are investigating. In earlier chapters you saw how reading can stimulate questions for research and inform professional understanding. When working towards formal accreditation, classroom teacher-researchers often find that their literature review is best woven throughout the research report, rather than being in a discrete literature review chapter.

I will tell you about the possibilities for taking action in my classroom research so that I can explain the importance of addressing the question 'What forms of knowledge might inform your decisions?'

I teach 4- to 12-year-old pupils with special education needs. My research question was 'How do I improve my teaching of pupils with difficulties in the area of oral language?' Many pupils with oral language difficulties in my workplace were not achieving according to their capabilities in curricular areas. For example, those who have dyslexia, dyscalculia, general learning difficulties, hearing problems, Down syndrome, Asperger syndrome, autistic tendencies, behaviour difficulties and speech and language disabilities may all experience communication difficulties. How they receive oral language information; how they interpret, understand and remember oral information and how they communicate with others are some of the communication stumbling blocks that can inhibit pupils' learning. My interest in oral language has general significance because existing research points to a correlation between oral language and academic achievement, For example, Nash-Wortham and Hunt (1993) found that language disorders are precursors to problems with reading, spelling and writing. Shaywitz and Shaywitz (2005) point out that the size of a child's vocabulary is one of the best predictors of comprehension, and that children with the biggest vocabularies tend to be the strongest readers.

These were the research possibilities that I set out: I will test, teach and retest. First I will test 14 pupils for areas of language difficulty with commercially available tests. Next I will teach lessons focusing on pupils' individual areas of difficultly. Then I will retest to evaluate the process and inform future teaching and learning. My time-line will be one month to gather data on pupils and test their language ability; next, three months of teaching interventions; then a one-month review, followed by a further three months of interventions and a final one month for review. I will allocate the remainder of the school year to writing up my report.

When I tried out these possibilities, I felt that the commercial testing process was very frustrating. Each test required pupils to continue with the testing tasks until they made a specific number of errors. I felt that in this form of testing I was spending days working in a way that was most discouraging for my pupils, whereas teaching for me is about helping pupils to succeed. I felt that the form of testing I had chosen pathologised my pupils rather than showed their capabilities. I was investigating my pupils' language skills as if they had a disease that I could treat. I was experiencing myself as a living contradiction, as was explained earlier in Chapter 4, because my values were being denied in the research actions I chose. But slowly things changed.

> During my research, I gathered information to show what I was doing in many ways. The test papers, test results and my interpretation of them, along with my journal, were part of my data-gathering methods. Anne was a senior work colleague who knew and understood my work context extremely well. I talked to her about administrating and scoring the tests accurately. We also interpreted the tests and how to best summarise each pupil's performance. The qualitative data that Anne and I had noted – such as physical behaviour or movements pupils made when they could not retrieve words – was invaluable in drawing coherent, concise and comprehensive conclusions from these tests.

I found my collaboration with Anne very affirming although, like many teachers conducting classroom-based research, I was initially very uneasy about bringing a colleague into my classroom. Anne was what research literature calls a critical friend or learning partner who could validate and critique my actions and my understanding of them. The qualitative and quantitative data from this testing process did not represent a comprehensive view of pupils' language ability, and the words qualitative and quantitative data were not part of the usual staffroom chat in my school. They were part of the new learning for me. I was moving from the professional language of teaching into the language of academics. Research literature can open up this new and essential vocabulary to teacher-researchers.

Armed with my new understanding that quantitative knowledge (where knowledge can be looked on as an object that can be measured) is not the only explanation of knowledge in a classroom setting, I revised my possible research plan. I decided to devise my personal teacher-made test for language in order to gain further information on why my pupils didn't communicate readily or successfully with peers. I wanted to find a way to investigate these aspects of language and use this content to inform my teaching. This was important because I believe that language is used to interpret and communicate meaning to oneself and the world as well as being a resource for literacy, thinking and learning as Addison Stone et al. (2006) have also found.

The questions 'Why are you doing this?', 'What motivates you?' and 'What forms of knowledge inform your decisions?' – some of which you have considered in previously – can also provide key learning opportunities within the research process. This phase seldom features in published theses and dissertations yet research literature is now taking it into account. For example, in an account of research projects in Lewisham, UK, Gewirtz et al. report that 'optimism and pessimism can be closely intertwined' (2009: 580) as researchers enthusiasm and research pressures collide. Cook describes how research is a mixture of mess and rigour and argues that the purpose of mess is to facilitate a turn towards new constructions of knowing that lead to transformation in practice. So rather than characterising messiness in research as negative, 'we need to celebrate the positive role it plays in creating depth and rigour' (2009: 291).

These authors are stressing the importance of including the messiness of classroom research in written reports because it demonstrates our engagement with the unlearning of previous thinking and habits and how this is replaced with new learning. In my research, for example, I realised slowly that action research is not just about describing actions and their effects or effectiveness. Writing up a classroom action research report requires explaining those descriptions about why the actions were taken. The specific actions that you choose need to be explained in relation to your work, school context and values that you have identified. Consequently you may need to explain issues such as policy, provisions, pedagogy and theories of learning within your context. When writing for accreditation purposes your explanations can include current theories from academic literature.

Reflective activity

To help you consider research possibilities, ask yourself:

- What actions might I take to show change in my situation or changes in my understanding?
- How can I show others that I reflected on my situation?
- List some ways I can collect information about these changes?
- How do my proposed actions relate to why I am doing this and what motivated me?

Making a plan to investigate the issue you have chosen

Planning actions to show change in your situation is the second phase of an action research process. You will make decisions about what kinds of data you might collect. The evaluation of an action research plan requires confidence in the quality and relevance of the data-gathering methods used. A further part of planning an action research project for your classroom is getting permission from all involved so that you can make your findings public. Over the next pages, I will use examples from my research to suggest how you might explain choices for collecting data, verifying and storing data, and discuss some ethical issues about collecting information from children and schools.

Collecting data

Trying out research possibilities and reflecting on them, as in the earlier part of this chapter, provides opportunities to check the appropriateness of the data collection process. As teacher-researchers there are three levels at which you can consider this:

- At a practice-based level, you can check if you are collecting data in ways that have relevance and are easily applicable without disrupting the educational opportunities of all involved.
- At a relevance level, your data collecting methods should be relevant to the context and conceptual frames of the issues you are investigating.
- At a value base level, you must decide the appropriateness of your research process and data collection methods. This level is core and relates to the value base you identified in earlier chapters.

In my research I found I could address these three levels by constantly reviewing my actions against my values and I would recommend this as an integral and ongoing part of choosing your actions and ways of collecting data. Here is an example from my research of what this looked like in practice.

My earlier descriptions of testing language were at odds with the value base of my research so I decided to video record and transcribe a five-minute conversation between individual pupils and myself. I analysed and summarised the transcript and invited further written comments on it from Anne, my critical friend, and from each pupil's class teacher. The pupils were also asked for their view on the process, after the test. I did not need to purchase any new teaching resources. My resources were the people involved in the testing, teaching and learning processes. Table 5.1 illustrates a clip from a transcript analysis where we discussed an elaborate picture from the pupil's favourite TV show.

Transcripts provided valuable data for reflection. I noted patterns that allowed me to identify specific pragmatic language difficulties. I was amazed at the amount of information I gleaned – knowledge about my interactive teaching style as well as pupils' learning abilities and difficulties. One example of this was my correction of the pupil on line 5 of the transcript shown in Table 5.1. Teachers might call what I did as thinking on the hoof and adapting my teaching accordingly. But writers on education, and in particular Schön (1995), call this reflection-in-action. Both phrases describe how teachers constantly modify teaching based on how learning is happening for pupils. The commentaries on the transcript were reflections-on-action, as described in earlier chapters. This form of data gathering and testing pupils' language offers a way to highlight pupils' abilities and was therefore in keeping with my values relating to equity, democracy and freedom, and wish to focus on ability rather than disability.

Table 5.1 Testing language in a conversation with a pupil

Transcript of session	My comments	Anne's comments	Class teacher's comments
1. Me: Good. Tell me all the things you see in the picture 2. Pupil: I see a swimming pool. 3. Me: Thank you. 4. Pupil: I see a . . . (gives a look indicating that she cannot remember) 5. Me: What would that be? . . . What could you use it for? 6. Pupil: Bucket and sade [sic]. 7. Me: Yes bucket and spade. Very good.	Pupil initially appeared well able for the task of naming, despite the mispronunciation in line 6. She has delays in retrieving words that she knows as in line 4. She uses a lot of physical movement to convey meaning.	Useful observations on pupil's physical reactions to her difficulties. Good correction technique.	I'm surprised that she didn't know bucket and spade immediately because she brought in her own ones for 'show and tell' last week.

In my reflections on selecting an appropriate testing tool, I realised another dilemma for teacher-researchers. Action research in the classroom that aims to enhance practice is not centred on finding theory that is a replicable and generalisable theory. As explained in Chapter 3, it is about putting the 'I' into research. For example, it is clear from my research question 'How do I improve my teaching of pupils with difficulties in the area of oral language?' that I have a very practical and personal focus on myself, as a teacher, and a specific group of pupils. My research lens had been focused on pupil learning up to this stage in my research. What I learned and want to communicate to you is that when you are conducting action research in your classroom with a view to enhancing your practice you too might shift the research lens and focus on you, the practitioner. How teacher-researchers can gather data and hold a focus on themselves can be problematic and involves looking at data verification and storage.

Verifying and storing data

To explain this I will return to the transcript example shown in Table 5.1. Combining the comments of research participant, a critical friend and class teacher was a way of verifying what I was doing. The pupil appeared to enjoy the test – he asked, 'Can we do it again?' Anne wrote, 'This was a fruitful language assessment and you used a context that was interesting and enjoyable for both of you.' The verification of my data in this way provided qualitative data of its accuracy and validity. Getting other perspectives on qualitative data so as to show its credibility by cross checking data (O'Donoghue and Punch 2003) is called triangulation. Triangulation can explain more fully the richness and complexity of what you describe because it is studied from more than one standpoint (Cohen, Manion and Morrison 2007) and so gives a more detailed and balanced picture (Altrichter *et al.* 2008).

The data collecting methods grow as the research process develops to suit the specific circumstances of the research site and participants. The lived experience of conducting the action research on one's teaching is a living process that can take on a life of its own – increasing the forms and amount of data you collect. By this second stage in my research I had a very large box of data containing individual pupil files, their learning profiles and attendance records, checklists of achievement, my journals, teaching notes, pictures, photos, videos, transcripts, questionnaires, meeting logs and records of verification meetings with my triangulation group and my critical friend, anecdotal records, self-assessment and peer assessment, test sheets, and records and surveys. I needed to look at storing my data in a methodical way to make it easier to retrieve and to show the authenticity of what I have done. For research accreditation purposes you should retain and store your data and records in a data archive. My data archive was a simple box with all items from my research dated and recorded on the index. Maintaining a data archive is recommended because it is essential so that others may check what you are claiming to have done. A data archive can be witnessed and a signed copy of the index of its contents can be appended to a research report.

Getting permission to use the data collected

There is a difference between formative testing to inform one's teaching and using that same data as evidence in a research project, which I will now explain. Testing and records of pupil's progress are part and parcel of teaching. Clear professional protocols exist around the storage of such data. But for accredited research purposes it is necessary for teacher-researchers to have permission from all those involved before making any of their research public. This may include school managers, the school head, colleagues and other education professionals who were involved in the research, as well as pupils and their parents. When carrying out my research I informed my school principal and board of management about my research aims, hopes and possible implications of my research for the school, and requested their permission to continue. I provided a signed ethical statement containing this information and they gave their written consent.

Universities have specific ethical requirements for research, which must be adhered to when submitting your research proposal and research report. Often a dilemma for teacher-researchers is that university ethics can be grounded in a scientific perspective, which refers to research subjects (participants) almost as if they were objects in laboratories. On occasion, I found it necessary to negotiate with a university ethical committee at an early stage in the research process in order to agree what wording and permissions would best suit both our purposes. My approach, as a teacher-researcher, was about adhering to my values around respect for the individual and their capabilities. I wanted to respect the dignity and privacy of all involved in my research (Bassey 1990, 1999) and my continual communication and interaction with research participants was an indicator of an ethical approach (Glesne and Peshkin 1992). Here is a description of how I dealt with ethical issues in a practical way, which may be of use to you.

> I presented the testing and lessons that I planned for my pupils as part of my research as part of their normal school work. I informed them that our discussions would help me to see how useful these new class ideas could be to them and other children. I asked the parents to agree that their child's work could be used as part of my research and invited them to view any data I planned to make public. Class teachers or parents could decide to withdraw pupils from the project, if any difficulties arose at any time. Colleagues were more cautious about giving consent. They feared they were being researched and very much appreciated the written ethical statement confirming their anonymity. I decided to withhold the name of my school and pupils from any published document. Where non-readers were involved in my research I made special arrangement; for example, parents and pupils co-signed the consent letter. To summarise, after discussing the implications of taking part in my research, I gave all involved in it a signed ethical statement and they gave their written consent. I gave participants copies of these documents and I appended their permissions to my thesis.

I have described a form of research which resonates with Pithouse, Mitchell and Weber (2009) who, in mapping out key features of self-study in teaching and teacher development, particularly about social action, draw on creative and participatory approaches. They highlight some of the ways in which the personal interconnects with the social and in so doing contributes to taking action. Their research illustrates the use of personal narrative and video documentary, in the context of their work with South African teachers, as they emphasise the potential particularly where ministries and faculties of education support self-study action research.

Reflective activity

Planning your research project, ask yourself:

- What kinds of data will I collect?
- How will I store my data?
- Who will be involved in my research?
- How will I get their permission to be part of my research?

Write a letter requesting permissions from those involved in your research. Think of the values you named in earlier chapters, and consider how to link them to the data gathering, plans and actions you have. Make an action plan using a mind-map with 'my concern/or question about my practice' at the centre and showing:

- possible actions you might take
- who will be involved in the research
- who will be involved in verifying data.

Carrying out your plan and gathering information to show how it is going

This is the third phase in an action research project. Feldman tells teacher-researchers to use their own experiences as a resource for their research and 'problematize their selves in their practice situations with the goal of reframing their beliefs and/ or practice' (Feldman 2002: 971). Because the form of action research in this book focuses on improvement at both personal and professional levels, we want to show explicitly the personal processes of reflection and enquiry within the research.

To provide a practical example of this, I will tell how I carried out my research plan and gathered information.

I taught two series of lessons to address two of the language difficulties (auditory memory and comprehension skills) that many of my pupils exhibited during my testing processes. First I taught a commercial programme, which claimed to develop auditory memory skills. Next I taught a series of teacher-designed lessons focused on comprehension skills that were directly linked to the curriculum because they were based on the mainstream class reading texts. These teaching interventions took place with groups of four pupils who were withdrawn from their main classes. Each of these interventions took place over three months and was followed by retesting.

As I taught these lessons, I reflected on the following questions, which you may find useful:

- What does this tell me about how my pupils learn?
- What do I learn about my own teaching from this action?

These questions relate to Feldman's ideas, described above. As a teacher-researcher you are no longer working within the isolation of your classroom. You are looking for ways:

- to make public what you are doing
- to show reflection and a personal critique of what you are doing
- to check your methods against the ontological and epistemological values that inform your research.

This final phase is critical in classroom action research because these values can become standards on which your research can be judged. Standards of judgement will be explained in the final part of this book. I will now explain the first two points with reference to my classroom research project.

Making public what you are doing

By the time my intervention lessons were completed I had gathered so much data that I thought I could never put it in order so as to write up a research report. The active participation of pupils in the process meant they too had an influence on the course of my research. Dadds and Hart (2001) use the term methodological inventiveness to describe how the research methods organically grow in this form of research. Their lovely idea holds out great possibilities for all engaged in classroom-based research for professional development.

But data overload is a common difficulty for teachers (Foulger 2010). For me, finding the relevance of the large amount of entries that I had made in my journal was particularly problematic. My journal notes were mainly cryptic, sometimes almost illegible and occasionally pencil sketches. They also included records of when things did not go according to plan. To help me make sense of all my journal notes I designed a personal cue card in the form of a bookmark to help me. A similar cue card might be a useful prompt in analysing your reflective journal for research purposes. On one side of the bookmark I wrote four cue questions:

1   Open: Am I open to my own learning?
2   Gap: Is this a gap between theory and my practice?
3   Challenge: Am I challenging my current practice?
4   Knowledge: Am I constructing knowledge?

I put coloured stickers on my journal with the appropriate letters – O, G, C or K from my cue card – as a quick reference. Some authors such as Altrichter *et al.* (2008) suggest strategies for listing, selecting and coding data but I prefer to consider all data that may have relevance to the education of participants. Using the bookmark cue I am analysing my thinking and the progression in my thinking as I study my professional work.

Showing reflection and personal critique of what you are doing

My teaching of the commercial programme for auditory memory reflected Skinner's (1954, 1957) definition of the laws of effect and exercise, which explained how stimulus, response and reinforcement brought about learning. In my journal I noted:

I am teaching in a behaviourist style where I choose the lesson content, instruct the pupils in the skills that I decide are important; when the pupils respond, I praise or correct them and continue with the next incremental phase of instruction.

Where were my values around respecting individual capabilities now? The discrepancies between my values and my practice caused a massive rethink in my research methods and of my teaching, which I tried to put into practice in the next series of lessons on comprehension.

To show the validity of the changes in my work and thinking I brought together a validation group of critical friends. They included my critical friend, some teachers, other researchers and someone familiar with current theories of language teaching from a university setting. A group of people who can critique and validate data in this way is called a validation group by McNiff (2002), among others, and a peer debriefing group by Cohen, Manion and Morrison (2007). Validation groups reinforce the idea that classroom research is not undertaken in isolation but requires collaboration for building new understanding through dialogue. Creating a validation group also provides a way to establish rigour in the research process, which will be addressed in Chapter 7.

In this third phase of classroom action research I have shown how you can take action, gather data and reflect on and in action. Ghaye (2011) has forensically examined various types of action – informed, committed, intentional, sustainable and positive. Although I agree with her hypothesis, my experiences are closer to Cook (2009), who suggests that 'significant additions to knowledge are characterised by departures from, as opposed to adherence to, method'. Cook concludes, however, that 'anarchic as it may initially seem – for rigorous research to take place, researchers need to both create and delve into the "messy area"' (Cook 2009: 289). As a teacher-researcher you will explain and justify the outcomes of your actions. Your judgement, experience and intuition are some of the lenses you will use. The reframing that takes place and new knowing has theoretical and practical significance as you will see in the next section.

Reflective activity

Taking action to research an issue in your practice, ask yourself:

- What actions did I take to show change in my situation or understanding?
- How do I show others what I have done?
- How do I show reflection on my actions and how are my actions critiqued?
- How do my data-collecting methods take into account the underlying values on which my work is premised?

Rigorously evaluating your research methods

In the fourth phase of an action research project teacher-researchers can evaluate the actions they have taken and the new learning that arises from it in three practical ways:

1 by testing it within a traditional scientific approach
2 by placing what you found before peers and asking for their evaluations
3 by testing your data against a wider educational community.

The significance of testing your findings in this wider forum will be explored in the final two chapters.

Dadds and Hart (2001) show how classroom action research can employ an eclectic mix of data-gathering methods – qualitative and qualitative – and this requires a variety of tests. You might consider informal as well as formal tests to establish a baseline or current level of educational performance as a basis for intervention. Within a traditional scientific approach, evaluation can be a simple comparison using standardised, criterion references or diagnostic testing before and after your research. Standardised tests allow us to make accurate comparisons with a specified group such as pupils of the same age or class on a national scale. On a criterion-referenced test the pupil's performance is not compared with that of others but with a pre-specified standard or criterion. A diagnostic test is designed to yield evidence on the particular aspects of learning in which the pupil is having difficulty. My initial testing of pupils' language, using commercial tests, is an example of a traditional scientific approach.

Accurate testing, however, does not always give us a full picture. Your methods will focus on you as a teacher within the research process so more than pupil baselines need to be evaluated.

A second level of evaluation of actions and reflections in classroom research is by peer review, which is an important part of the academic research process of legitimating and validating. For example getting a paper published in a peer reviewed journal carries a lot of weight, and a viva where candidates are seeking to have research validated also includes the idea of peer review. Not all teacher-researchers are seeking academic accreditation and for those teachers, finding a practical form of peer review to evaluate their research can pose problems. I will tell you about how my pupils directed me towards a peer review process during lessons on auditory memory – one of the key difficulties we worked on.

My pupils drew pictures to depict how they each remembered things best. When my pupils presented and explained their pictures to each other, they drew comparisons with their differing findings. One pupil commented,

> We do it different. Xavier and Yuri make notes to remember but I don't. Zoe doesn't either. Zoe and me make a picture in our heads. Zoe makes like a video with her pictures, but my pictures are separate like in an album.
>
> Given the enjoyment and confidence they experienced from sharing their new knowledge, it wasn't surprising when one pupil suggested, 'What about telling the rest of my class about this?' Class teachers gave them time to describe and explain their pictures to the other 30 pupils in their mainstream classes. I accompanied them and videoed these interactions. After each presentation, my pupils fielded questions with assuredness.

These critiques were based on experiential and practical learning that had relevance to the context in which the research was taking place. The expanded research circle meant that I had to negotiate additional permissions from more mainstream pupils and teachers. In earlier parts of this book other ideas for peer review have been explained, such as critical friends and triangulation validation groups. These are academically accepted forms of verification of data, but they are also ways in which you can create new knowledge within reflective discussions and critique.

A further testing of research actions can take place in the wider school community. Here is a research vignette and in it I am asking if my research activities could change professional practice or knowledge.

> Some staff members had not heard presentations from the pupil so they were invited to my classroom to hear the pupils explain their memory strategies. At the end of their presentations teachers and pupils commented. One pupil remarked how he enjoyed the experience of talking to a teacher like that. He said, 'I was a bit scared but I thought it would be a good idea 'cos they would know how to help me remember things.'
>
> Teachers were similarly surprised at what they learned. One stated, 'I couldn't believe how confident William [pupil] was and how clearly he explained about how he understood and remembered things.'

Globally, evaluation of self-study action research has been shown to contribute to teachers' professional development. Bustingorry's research in South America explains how for teachers the constant practice of action research cycles around pedagogical practice – planning, action, observation and reflection – 'influenced positively the development of the professional autonomy of the teachers involved in the research' (2008: 418). She reports improvement at both the theoretical level and practice level in that teachers were more autonomous in adapting to students' learning needs.

In the final section of this chapter I will explain a further test of data by reflecting on the potential of new learning developed through your actions and reflections to influence further developments in your classroom and in the wider education community.

Reflective activity

Evaluating your research approach, ask yourself:

- What do my actions tell me about how my pupils learn?
- What do I learn about my own teaching from my action?
- How can I show that my research actions are related to the underlying values on which my work is premised?

Can your research influence future actions or understandings?

This question takes us to the last phase in an action research project. The phases addressed in this chapter are:

- setting out some possibilities to show how you might research a professional issue of interest to you
- making a plan to investigate the issue you have chosen with a view to improvement
- carrying out your plan and gathering information to show how it is going
- rigorously evaluating your research methods
- establishing if your research can influence future actions or understanding.

These phases form a cyclical process – an action-reflection research cycle of planning, acting, reflecting, evaluating and deciding on the next areas to investigate. Teacher-researchers can enjoy this research approach because it mirrors the process of teaching daily where you can plan what to teach and how to teach it, teach the lessons, think about how the lessons went and test what pupils have learned, and finally plan your next lesson based on your findings. This five-phase cycle represents a practical approach to classroom research and can be linked to the work of Stenhouse (1975) and Wragg (1983), among others, who tried to encourage teachers to take an active role in educational research. Rephrasing the five-phase action research process into questions has recently also gained in popularity, as in the writings of Whitehead (1989), McNiff and Whitehead (2009; 2010) and McNiff (2010).

The final phase of the research cycle is about relating your actions and reflections to future possibilities, and examining your research episodes for demonstrations of how you have influenced the wider education community's knowledge and practice. This educative influence is said by McNiff and Whitehead (2010) to be about engaging in collaborative practices to create cultures of inquiry when we share our knowledge, disseminate our ideas, and encourage others to do the same. Teachers often find it easy to share the tips and tricks of their teachers' craft such as useful resources, websites and texts, but are more reticent in putting their findings before colleagues. I was one of those teachers. But by examining my influence on the education of each participant in my research I found that I could begin to see that my research had importance. For me the key participants were pupils, the school staff and myself. First, I looked at what was different for my pupils and how that could possibly change things in the future.

> My pupils had become co-researchers during my research project. They were conducting personal mini action research projects about their ways of comprehending and remembering. They had become knowers of their own ways of learning and had made a contribution to the learning of others in our school.

Next I looked for examples of change in practice. I had made giant shifts in how I taught and thought during the action research process. I had moved from a behaviourist style of teaching and learning to an interactive community of learning where all involved were sharing their ideas as they learned together. Next I considered how this had impacted on staff. Here is one example of the influence of my research actions when staff heard my pupils explain their new learning.

> Teachers said:
>
> > The combination of the children's voices and your reflections on their learning let us see how you support learning in your class.
> >
> > I and the other teachers were learning from the lived experiences of you and your pupils.
> >
> > The very simple yet multi-layered idea of asking pupils themselves how they remember, and the realisation that these children have a very clear sense of the ways that work for them, in remembering and answering comprehension questions, struck me very forcibly. Thanks.
> >
> > Having heard this I will do things differently in the future.

As for me, I have had a learning experience that will influence my future as a professional. I have engaged in educational research based on me and my practice. I plan to continue this form of self-evaluation at a practical and conceptual level because it provides me with a practical approach to the marrying of theory and practice. I plan to continue enhancing practice through classroom research because it allows the research of non-stop lived experiences of teaching to coalesce.

The outward expression of the educational influence of your research can lie in investigating its relevance for your research for all its participants – pupils, teachers and school community. This can be an empowering experience for many teacher-researchers.

I hope you will find that working through the five stages of an action research cycle is satisfying, but you may find that structuring what happened into a written report especially for academic accreditation is problematic. This is a frequent difficulty because, as Winter says, writing research reports is an attempt 'to do justice to the always frustrating relationship between the linear sequence of words on a page, the infinite complexities of experience, and the desire to elucidate a wider significance from particular events' (2002: 25). Written academic research reports often presume a transmission model of knowledge. In contrast, classroom research towards enhancing practice, as described in this book, includes multiple understandings and ways of creating knowledge. Using live evidence, such as digital media, web pages and DVD in reports, as well as more traditional data-gathering methods, is slowly gaining in popularity and helps communicate the lived reality of being a teacher-researcher.

Chapter summary

Chapter 5 explored a five-staged approach to gathering information to show the situation as it was and evolved during your research. This staged approach required cycles of acting, data gathering and reflecting on what is happening. I have described various techniques for gathering data that I used during my classroom research, including issues around validity and ethics. The many data-gathering approaches that I have described represent a dynamic approach to developing new learning for the teaching professions. I hope that my descriptions help you in researching the issues that you have identified in your professional setting and that the reflective activities encourage you to take action in your work context.

The underpinning impetus for actions and choice of data-gathering methods in classroom action research are the ontological and epistemological values that teacher-researchers hold. In my research I have gone about showing research in my work situation that was democratic as it enabled the participation of all. It was also equitable as it acknowledged people's worth. It was liberating in providing opportunities learners to express their own views and finally it was life-enhancing because it enabled all involved to move towards their potential. In Chapter 6 I will explain the overall reasons why I chose this form of research.

Some research and theoretical insights from my practice

Where teachers are enabled to research their own practice, they are better able to own their findings and become 'producers of knowledge' and 'redistribution of autonomy and judgement' (Stenhouse 1983: 166).

For classroom action research to integrate enhancement of practice and new research knowledge 'we must provide honest accounts of that process and incorporate mess as an integral part of a rigorous approach' (Cook 2009).

Teacher research has transformative potential. Postholm (2009) reports that action research in Norway is called research and development (R&D): research and development are conducted at the same time.

Classroom action research will be meaningful and productive when it goes 'beyond providing tools and techniques of knowledge creation and [comes] to understand "the subjectivities and identities of both teachers and academics"' (Gewirtz *et al.* 2009). This requires the foregrounding of the value of integrating research into educational practice as a source of personal and institutional development and less emphasis on conventional academic criteria and forms of tuition. This book has been structured to demonstrate this approach with the criteria for making claims to new knowledge in the final section.

There may need to be a shift in ownership and control of research. For example, can teacher-researchers control the dissemination of their research since their research is adding to the knowledge base of their profession rather than being solely the property of academia? In the final part of the book we will examine what counts as legitimate research.

Further reading

Altrichter, H., Feldman, A., Posch, P. and Somekh, B. (2008) *Teachers Investigate their Work: An Introduction to Action Research across the Professions*, 2nd edn, London: Routledge.
A guide to many research methods for educators and other professionals who aim to investigate their practice in order to improve it.

Kincheloe, J.L. (2003) *Teachers as Researchers: Qualitative Inquiry as a Path to Empowerment*, 2nd edn, Oxton and New York: Routledge.
Beginning with a definition of work, and its implications for understanding the ethics of teaching and learning, the book investigates how research can support teachers in understanding their world and gaining power over it.

McNiff, J. and Whitehead, J. (2010) *You and Your Action Research Project*, 3rd edn, London: RoutledgeFalmer.
Models a practice of action research with case studies from a variety of disciplines.

Chapter 6

Finding a research methodology

This chapter explores:

- how to choose an overall research methodology
- three educational research paradigms
- examples of my search for an appropriate methodology for my classroom research
- some exercises to help you document your actions and research on the educational research paradigms.

Introduction

The previous chapter described how you might research changes in your teaching or your understanding of it. This chapter looks at the bigger picture of how research methodologies can help you as a teacher-researcher to formalise your actions, reflections and evaluations. As well as a classroom friendly research approach, you may also be looking for a methodology that can lead to postgraduate level accreditation and could have the potential to influence policy decision making. An overall approach to research is called a methodology or a paradigm, as I will now explain.

An explanation of your research methodology is an integral part of many research reports. Traditionally the methodology is dictated by the subject being researched and since this book explains a form of classroom research to enhance practice, the methodology must reflect the complexities of real classrooms and teaching. It took me a long time to decide on a research methodology that would allow me to examine changes that I was making in my teaching. I found it difficult to find a research methodology to suit my study of how I teach pupils with difficulties in language. So, in this chapter, instead of suggesting a prescriptive methodology for classroom research that aims to improve practice, I explain my journey towards an appropriate paradigm, which may help you as you structure your plan. During this journey I explore three major paradigms – empirical, interpretive and action research. Bassey explains research paradigms as a 'network of coherent ideas about the nature of the world and the functions of researchers, which [is] adhered to by a group of researchers, conditions their thinking and underpins their research actions' (Bassey 1990: 8). In this chapter I use four questions, which reflect Bassey's (1990) ideas, to investigate the appropriateness of each paradigm for me and hope you will find these questions useful when deciding on your methodology.

The first two questions link the relevance of a research paradigm to me, my understanding of my world and my research by asking:

1   Where am I placed as a professional within the paradigm?
2   Does it allow me to think professionally, act and reflect on my practice?

The remaining two questions link each paradigm to professional development by examining how the underpinning values of the paradigm inform my thinking during my research and how they further influenced the writing of my research report:

3   Can the paradigm increase my autonomy as a professional?
4   Can the paradigm help me contribute to the knowledge base of the teaching profession?

Each of these questions enabled me, and hopefully will guide you, to move towards a paradigm that is suitable for researching with the vulnerable young people with whom we work. I explore some aspects of the main research paradigms on the questions I have outlined above:

- empirical research
- interpretive research
- action research.

I discuss each of them with examples from my research and explain how I visualised each paradigm. The chapter includes some activities that may help you write up your research project.

Empirical research

Hitchcock and Hughes (1995) explain that your way of being in the world (ontology) colours your understanding of knowledge (epistemology) and who are considered valid knowers. This in turn influences your choice of methodology and you can begin to explore the value base that underpins it and ask about your position as a professional within empirical research.

Where am I placed as a professional within empirical research?

My love of science coloured how I pictured my world when I began my research. My interest in objective reality and knowledge, expressed as factual statements, epitomises the empirical paradigm. This paradigm is about testing a hypothesis using observation and experiment – a scientific understanding of the world. Cohen, Manion and Morrison (2007), when talking about this methodology, trace the origins of a scientific search for truth back to Aristotle in ancient Greece. The empirical paradigm is also called a scientific, positive, technical or theoretical research paradigm according to Carr and Kemmis (1986), Bassey (1990) and Cohen, Manion and Morrison (2007). It is underpinned by the idea that the only authentic knowledge is that based on sense experience and positive verification. It is a research format that is easily explained, consistent and non-negotiable.

You too may be interested in observable cause and effect explanations, in consistency and generalisability where your research findings can be applied in other settings. To establish what your role is as a teacher-researcher in this paradigm, let us look at an example from an initial phase of my research.

> I wanted to develop a testing system suitable for teachers of pupils who have difficulties in language. I thought that if I could find literatures to tell me all the sub-skills of language, and a measuring scale to measure those skills, I could provide an intervention for the pupils and measure any improvements.

As an empirical researcher, I am the arbiter of what happens and what counts as knowledge in researching a language programme for my pupils. The picture in my mind of an empirical approach, or my visual metaphor, was that of books, a measuring scale and me delivering an intervention programme. My thinking was influenced by my desire for certainty, measurement and provability, which in turn influenced my research choices. I was looking for the correct answer or answers.

Does an empirical methodology allow me to think professionally, and act and reflect on my practice?

Researchers using this methodology create new knowledge about education and educators, so they are the valid knowers who can observe and theorise from their observations of educators' actions. They may generate statistical generalisations from what they observe. As Alexander (2006) says, these statistical generalisations state regularities that control behaviour regardless of human choices. This, in turn, could imply that teachers are expected to apply the theories of others to their practice – a transmission form of knowledge.

Within this paradigm, where theories are generated by outsider researchers, you as a teaching professional could be positioned as an implementer of the theories of others rather than as a capable theorist in your own right. For example, teachers like me who are engaged in special education can become functionaries who implement theories from other research fields such as medicine, psychiatry, psychology and various therapies.

I consider that the application of theory to practice is more difficult than it sounds and I wrote about this in my journal as follows:

> During many professional development courses I have noted great ideas that I intended to apply to my teaching. Often these great notes gathered dust on my book shelves where they sat alongside refereed journals rather than helping me to change how I teach.

Yet when structured developmental programmes, designed to address pupils' specific needs, have been researched in a scientific way, teachers can gain useful information, which can be the basis of their programme selection decisions. However, it seems to me that an empirical approach could not contribute to answering research questions like 'How do I improve..?' (Research diary 14 February 2006)

Can empirical research increase my autonomy as a professional?

Many teachers may feel overwhelmed by assessments, policies and bureaucratic directives coming from educational authorities. Yet as teachers we can counter these situations by becoming autonomous professionals who can take responsibility for our actions by questioning how and why we engage in good professional practice (Teaching Council of Ireland 2009). I felt that I was taking responsibility when I initially chose commercial tests and programmes. These programmes positioned knowledge as measured and objective. But this perspective was at odds with what was happening in my teaching and with my professional values around education. For example, when I deliver the same lesson content (or box of knowledge) to a group of pupils, they may come to understand and use what I have taught them in very different ways. There is always a personal element in knowledge creation in the classroom.

A quantitative understanding of knowledge where knowledge is looked on as an object that can be measured is not the only explanation of knowledge in a classroom research setting. I have felt that an empirical methodology has clashed with my values as a professional in some of the standard ways in which validity is checked. This paradigm involves the idea of changing only one variable at a time, the use of control groups, placebo and/or blind testing. Despite their importance to the accuracy of the research I am concerned with the respect afforded to the research participants, especially since in my research I was looking at ideas around equity, democracy and freedom, and focusing on ability rather than disability of the individual learner. Like me, you may find there is a clash between the values you have identified in previous chapters and knowledge expressed in definitive statements, as required in an empirical research methodology. If you continued only with this methodology you might need to check who gains directly from these regulatory features in research and knowledge, what the educational advantages for pupils in a control group are, who gains from the repetition of the same research process to satisfy statistical needs, and how this methodology contributes to teachers' professional autonomy.

Unfortunately an empirical methodology does not increase teacher autonomy because our personal teacher craft and expertise are filtered out in favour of the ideal of objectivity within an empirical paradigm. Personally I don't find that this approach to research increases my personal professional autonomy. You may not agree with my conclusions but it is worth considering whether this paradigm improves your professional knowledge base.

Can empirical research help me contribute to the knowledge base of the teaching profession?

What is the real-life understanding of the knowledge base of teaching? The Teaching Council of Ireland (2009) says that teaching is not a set of discrete skills but is a holistic endeavour. The professional ontological base of teaching focuses on empowerment and on the development of individuals, for example, curricula cite aims such as students reaching their potential (Ireland, DES 1999). This suggests a clash at a conceptual level between the values around knowledge creation in the teaching profession and knowledge as represented within empirical research. The knowledge base for us, as professional teachers, does not only mean boxable quantities of (curricular) information being absorbed by students as I had visualised it at the beginning of this section. It is a much broader concept.

In much empirical educational research the researcher is reporting on the work as an external observer who is expected to be objective. Reports of this form of research avoid the words 'I', 'me' or 'my' and are written in the third person. Even the visual metaphor that I used earlier in this chapter to represent an empirical research approach put the 'I' in the picture as a functionary, a deliverer of tests and interventions as in the commercial tests and lessons.

An empirical approach can definitely contribute to the knowledge base of the teaching profession when knowledge is understood only as statistically verifiable facts, objective realities and absolute truths, and where experiments and conclusions can be replicated.

In my research I found that much of the educational research in my field, which was available in refereed journals, was about describing, interpreting and explaining what was happening without trying to change anything. The authors describe the context and concepts under investigation. The context description might include historical, policy or provision issues while the concepts reference existing literatures and theories. Their discussions and findings more often highlight the need for further research rather than action, or decisions about how to change or improve teaching. These reports are not designed to give any understanding of the process of changing your practice because they are not focusing on process but on verifiable facts.

To summarise, an empirical paradigm offers teachers a useful methodology for gaining knowledge about teaching and facts to inform teaching. The research process is preordained, so it prevents researchers 'from engaging and experiencing ownership in the research process' (Donham, Heinrich and Bostwick 2010: 8). However, classroom research from your professional perspective as a teacher-researcher is about commitment to your work, concern about how your work is progressing, consideration of possibilities for change, and collaboration in acting on these possibilities and evaluating changes. So an empirical paradigm appears not to suit teacher-researchers but aspects of this paradigm can help you develop effective classroom-based research.

Reflective activity

In order to develop an understanding of research methodology, choose a published research article in your field of interest and consider:

- What is the epistemological perspective of the researcher?
- What is the ontological perspective of the researcher?

Interpretive research

An interpretive research methodology seems to have been developed by researchers who, like me, were no longer happy with the perspective empirical research offered on the world. Cohen, Manion and Morrison (2007) and Guba and Lincoln (2005) call it a post-positivist paradigm to address the criticisms of the positivist paradigm of empirical research. Bassey (1999) calls it an evaluative methodology because it is not concerned with scientific knowledge alone but it enables researchers to act as theorists who try to describe, interpret and explain what is happening, while also making value judgements such as in case studies and ethnography. Carr and Kemmis (1986) refer to it as practical and many fields of research have found it useful so that it has become known under various names such as phenomenology, ethno-methodological, hermeneutics and social anthropology.

Where am I placed as a professional within interpretive research?

In this question I am asking what the world view of an interpretive researcher is. I can best explain it with an interpretative example from my own research when I videoed my language classes. A colleague and I watched the video and interpreted what was happening.

As I watched I was trying to analyse how the pupils learned. It struck me how body language, eye-contact and enabling language, as well as seating and a pleasant environment, can encourage learning. I wondered if I could find a research format to record or chart such relational teacher–learner qualities. In addition, the teacher and pupils were not static like easily tabulated facts. They were multi-faceted, multi-talented, changing, thinking and transforming beings. My colleague and I sat chatting, later that evening, about different pupils and interpreted how they had reacted to me, as their teacher, to others in the class, to the visual cues provided by me and so on. I noted in my diary that the qualitative data gleaned through my observations, and discussion and interpretation yielded great insights.

As in this example, an interpretive methodology offers teacher-researchers a more natural approach to knowledge and organic growth-learning. As Lather (2006) pointed out, it is co-operative, interactive and humanistic. So the world view that supports this methodology emphasises the importance of different ways of knowing and dialogue.

The visual metaphor I use to explain how I am positioned within an interpretive paradigm sees me (or you as a teacher-researcher) in a commentary box with co-commentators describing and analysing what is happening on the field of play at a football match. We have an overview of the action and what is happening in the rest of the pitch and stadium. We are positioned so that we can observe, interpret and comment.

An interpretive methodology allows you, or me, to make explicit what is implicit in the classroom but in my visual metaphor I cannot be a player on the field as well as a commentator. Similarly, as a teacher-researcher, you may want to take part in the action being observed but cannot. Despite this, an interpretive approach could add to your conceptualisation of your actions and you can explore this in the next question.

Does an interpretive methodology allow me to think professionally, and act and reflect on my practice?

An interpretive research approach can add to professional understanding because the teaching and learning process can be observed, interpreted and commented on. Then, through reading the researcher's descriptions, other teachers can empathise and identify with the interpretations presented of lived reality of your teaching situation.

How can you as a teacher-researcher ensure the validity of your commentaries? Like me, you may find that your co-commentators can prevent your interpretations from becoming too subjective or unreliable. Subjectivity and unreliability are possible negatives in an interpretive methodology, according to Croll (1986). Díaz Andrade (2009) talks of ways to ensure validity – construct validity, internal validity and external validity. Construct validity is about maintaining data and a data archive, so that you have a chain of data from multiple sources in order to present a persuasive account. Those reviewing your interpretive account might disagree with your conclusions or interpretations but not with the factual accuracy of your data. Internal and external validity is about matching patterns of behaviour that you observe and explaining them in relation to other possible explanations and theories. Here is an example from my research.

> When I taught the series of lessons, as I have described in Chapter 5, I analysed the data using an interpretive approach. The data included entries from my reflective journal as well as comments from colleagues who had viewed the lessons and the data I gathered.

Bell (1993) echoes some of these ideas on researching classroom practice when she says that useful though grids, forms and checklists are they cannot take account of emotions, tensions and hidden agendas which teachers know exist. An interpretive approach offers you a co-operative research lens, where together with others you can create new theories on what you observed. In my fictive box, you and your fellow commentators and your public in television land have an opportunity to view what happens in your teaching – a feature which is not possible in a solely empirical approach.

Returning to my visual metaphor for an interpretive paradigm, I and my fellow commentators are not the team trainers, coaches or managers so we do not have a direct impact on how the team plays. When classroom research is undertaken using an interpretive approach, as I have described it, there is no direct effect on practice. Those involved in the observation process may link what they see to existing theories. Readers may be influenced by the research evaluations but my next task is to find out whether this methodology contributes to teacher autonomy and the realisation of teacher values in research and practice.

Can interpretive research increase my autonomy as a professional?

In empirical research there is a large divide between teacher and researcher in that one cannot be simultaneously the researcher and the object of the research. An interpretive approach, on the other hand, gives the teacher-researcher a degree of autonomy in that we can be both a researcher and a teacher. The values that underpin the interpretive paradigm include, first, a shift in who are valued as knowers within the teaching and research process. Looking at the triangulation process of validation, which I described above, it is easy to see who are considered valid knowers. Those involved in the triangulation are like your fellow commentators, who were with you in the commentary box in my visual metaphor for an interpretive approach to research. As a co-commentator you are positioned as knower along with others in the interpretation of practice.

The co-operative review process, which is a key element in an interpretive approach, gives teacher-researchers opportunities to reflect on their practice. But, educational interpretive research often involves a researcher from outside the research context identifying a knowledge gap or practice-based gap, using observations, interviews, questionnaires, surveys and statistics to evaluate (or interpret) a situation. When this happens, the authentic voice of the practitioner – the researched – can sometimes either be silenced or filtered through the interpretation of the spectator researcher.

Similar to Postholm (2009), I found that an interpretive paradigm can encourage a theoretical stance, in that theory can help teachers describe why things are as they are in their context. Theory can become a tool to help teachers to 'argue for, understand and see further possibilities in their teaching' (2009: 561). But, as in this book, practice must come first and then be united with theory in interpretive discussions so that you are bringing theory and practice together.

This said, an interpretive research methodology supports the view that researchers construct their own knowledge (Bassey 1990). So the next question is about how an interpretive research approach increases our knowledge as a teaching profession.

Can interpretive research help me contribute to the knowledge base of the teaching profession?

Carrying out interpretive research can be enjoyable and informative. I found this to be the case because it located me, as a researcher, in the tensions of the various fields of knowledge that exist in the teaching profession. It helped me focus on teaching and learning processes. For example, our triangulation conversations mirrored the discourse of this methodology, which is dialogical. It offers an open-minded approach where we can debate our varying perspectives. Rather than an empirical research paradigm that aims to find a single truth, you can engage with the idea of holding many truths.

You might wonder how an interpretive methodology supports the ideas of many truths. The key is in the ontological values that underpin this paradigm. Let us return to being in the commentators' box at football match. You have a powerful vantage point. Your report will open up an interpretation of classroom life for research because of the forms of data you can present and the validation processes. Here is a short description from my research.

I adopted an interpretive methodology in order to try to evaluate the progress of my pupils with language difficulties. I was studying my pupils. They were the objects of my research. A classroom observation approach meant that I could gather data in the form of field-notes (my journal, lesson notes, pupil portfolios of work completed and so on), conversations, transcriptions, observations, and even photos and videos for validation purposes, as part of its methodology.

Lather (2006) talks of the capacity for interpretive approaches to demonstrate the layering complexities of a scenario and its usefulness in foregrounding problems. This capacity can help you to gain new knowledge about the complexity of the world of teaching and learning. It is also about watching people in action and interpreting it. Hitchcock and Hughes (1995) referred to interpretive research as a people science. An interpretive report can be written either in the third or first person. This methodology can provide new knowledge for the teaching profession and can be relevant at both a practice and personal level.

In summary, an interpretive paradigm may suit the professional ontological perspectives that many teachers hold. It can give you information that is relevant to your teaching and your particular circumstances. The interpretive approach with which I planned to investigate my pupils, who had specific language difficulties, added two new levels of understanding to my search for an appropriate research methodology:

1   An interpretive methodology can interpret practice; however, my research aims were to improve practice.
2   I valued a pupil-centred approach in my teaching and I had not yet found a methodology that similarly valued research participants.

Reflective activity

To examine the relevance of methodology to practice, choose a published case study article and consider:

• How does it make teachers more autonomous?
• How does it generate new knowledge for teachers?

Action research

I am using the term action research to describe a methodology for classroom research and professional development that I found helpful in investigating and improving my practice. As I describe how I came to choose this research approach you will see that it is based in values that motivate many educators. By trying this methodology you too can create living personal theories that have current relevance in your classroom. I will begin my explanation for choosing an action research methodology with asking about my position as a professional within an action research paradigm.

Where am I placed as a professional within an action research paradigm?

This question is about the world view that underpins action research. I would agree with Carr and Kemmis (1986) who said that action research involves taking action (action) in order to find out what is not known (research) and in so doing to bring about improvements. The reasoning behind this research approach is that the individuals are seeking to live according to their core values in their teaching. Their research accounts explain their educational influence on students and on their wider community. See the websites of Educational Action Research in Ireland (<http://www.eari.ie>), Jean McNiff (<http://www.jeanmcniff.com>) and Jack Whitehead (<http://www.actionresearch.net>).

Here, I want to acknowledge that there are many forms of action research and it has changed and developed its emphasis over time. Because of its adaptability to research problems and actions it will probably continue to evolve. Early action researchers struggled – as I have – to be free from the positivist paradigm as they attempted to solve curriculum problems through a scientific work ethic. Lewin (1948) presented an approach to action research with cycles of analysis, fact-finding, conceptualisation, planning, implementation and evaluation of actions. Gradually professional development became a focus for much action research where researchers often challenged themselves, the situation and others in the belief that they need to understand the situation in order to change. Carr and Kemmis (1986) called this form of action research an emancipatory paradigm. Whitehead (1989) introduced the living theory approach to action research, where individuals could generate their own valid explanations of their educational influences in learning enquiries which ask 'How am I improving what I am doing?' (Whitehead 2011: 1). Since then ideas of the researcher being the research field have come to the fore (McDonagh 2009). Loughran (2010) states that the self-study action research movement emerged in the 1990s. According to Wilcox, Watson and Patterson (2004), this approach allows a practitioner to engage in a critical enquiry that contributes to their own capacity for expert and caring practice. Samaras and Freese suggest that self-study is about how 'improving one's practice benefits the larger broader practice of the advancement of knowledge in teaching and the educational system' (2006: 14).

In this book our focus is not on action research for institutional change per se, although this may occur. The examples drawn from our research reports show how we engaged in self-studies of our own practice in order to improve what we were doing, understand our reasons for it, and thereby personalise our professional development through undertaking classroom-based research in our own contexts.

In self-study action research you can be at the heart of the action and at the heart of the research. You are both a teacher and a researcher in this form of living theory action research methodology as Whitehead and McNiff (2006) have explained it. In my own research the analogy of being positioned as a heart in an action research methodology is about me, as teacher-researcher, being a life-force influence in a number of areas:

- The energy of knowledge is flowing freely around me and my students.
- I am a life-force allowing all research participants to have autonomy as well as to partake in the research.
- It is a way of living. I am in a non-stop cycle of action and reflection. Action researchers who commit to this form of research may live it all their lives.

I will explain these ideas in my examination of the three questions that follow.

Does action research allow me to think professionally, act and reflect on how values inform my practice?

There are many visual metaphors in the literature around action research. Schön (1995) talks about the swampy lowlands of practice-based research in contrast to the lofty ground of academia. Stenhouse (1975) talks of a spiral of action and reflection. McNiff (2005) uses the idea of the generative transformational nature of evolutionary processes to represent educational enquiries. Her image is that the beginning (as in the life of growing plants) 'holds its own future already latent within itself, and each living form has the transformational capacity to transform itself endlessly into new versions of itself' (2005: 157). Her representation reminds me of the ongoing nature of action research enquiries. The picture in my mind's eye for the living classroom, self-study action research approach that this book explains is of waves. I used this visual metaphor of waves to help me to structure my written research report into the necessary format for academic accreditation. I share it with you as a guide for when you are writing up your account of the fluid five-staged approach that you worked on in Chapter 5.

In my picture of this methodology, I see myself as a person standing in the sea of life, water up to my waist, waves and currents tugging at me. The waves gather momentum and change things dramatically as I work my way through my research (McDonagh 2009).

Here is a vignette from the final stage of my classroom research to explain this visual metaphor in practical terms. I am teaching comprehension – the pupils' second area of identified difficulty. In the first wave I felt the power of practical curricular requirements and of policy commitments to the inclusion of pupils with learning difficulties.

I decided to tackle a difficulty that my pupils had in answering higher- and lower-order questions on a piece of class text. We read a piece of text together and I asked them to compose a lower order question about it, beginning 'who', 'what', 'when' or 'where'. I was using a class text so that my pupils could be included more fully in their mainstream homework and I was working on oral comprehension rather than written comprehension to differentiate the curriculum for them.

In the second wave I experienced the clash between work and my life values where pupils perceived teachers as gatekeepers of knowledge. Yet I saw pupils as capable individuals who could create their own knowledge. In the next extract I describe how they did so by developing personal comprehension strategies.

Pupils worked in pairs on the challenge of creating questions and then asked the rest of the group to respond to the questions they composed. They were delighted to 'be the teacher' asking questions. At this stage the pupils were still positioning me as the gatekeeper of knowledge. Having congratulated them I asked them to explain to each other how they found the answers. When asked a question that began 'where', one pupil said, 'I looked for capitals 'cos places names start with them.' Another said, 'I looked for "in" because usually you are in somewhere.' Pupils came up with personal strategies to answer questions. I asked the pupils to record their new knowledge by drawing a cue-card to help them remember their strategy.

I reflected that my pupils were both creating and sharing knowledge that was new to them.

In the third wave I felt the tug of war between traditional educational theory and my practice. By this I mean that my work as a teacher is influenced by traditional theories of teaching, learning and language, which can often be of limited practical use. So I was seeking a form of theory, generated from my living practice, which also has the potential to contribute to a knowledge base for teachers (Zeichner 2007). Here is an example of how theory began to grow from within my practice.

Our next class surprised me. The pupils had their cue card in front of them. We read class texts and repeated the question-creating activity. George said, 'I want to try James' way.' The others followed George's example and conducted a minor piece of action research to find the strategy that worked best for each of them. By the end of this session they had six strategies, which they each had investigated and decided was the most efficient for them personally. Their preferences were quite different. For example the visual learners like George preferred visual strategies like looking for capitals, while others preferred auditory strategies like listening for cue words such as 'in' or 'at'. Even more amazing was the fact that they began to critique each other's choices. Each pupil had put forward a theory, which was being publicly critiqued by the group.

The fourth wave represents the successes and failures of my teaching, which were also documented in my research, and what I learned from them. My pupils had devised and recorded their personal theories. I recorded in my own journal, 'We are co-creators of knowledge. We have created some knowledge about the skills or strategies for comprehension. How can we take action? How can we share this?'

During the course of my research and the writing up of my report, the four waves combined to gather sufficient momentum to generate a fifth wave – a tidal wave of learning. These four waves intermingled. This intermingling is my way of portraying how I perceive myself as part of a complex and ever-changing reality which I cannot step outside of. The waves transformed all within their living flood.

Again I reflected that in parallel to my pupils' mini research study, I was conducting my own research. I had previously followed the thinking in research literature that comprehension skills need to be explicitly taught (Gersten *et al.* 2001). I had committed myself to the idea of practitioners as implementers of the theories of others when I considered laminating and reusing the skill cue cards that the pupils devised. But the research episode shows how I came to reposition my understanding of knowledge. Rather than as a reifiable commodity, I saw it now as personal and created within a community of learning. This was the epistemological base of my research stance – knowledge as personal yet relational, and created through dialogue. Another key value in my approach is that of respect for the capability of all to learn.

With the aid of this metaphor you can reflect on the relevance of this methodology for teacher-researchers. Action research can give you an opportunity to examine the gap between theory in your field of research and your practice, to challenge your current practice, to construct knowledge, to be open to your own learning. This methodology can provide you with opportunities to take responsibility for your actions by questioning how and why you can engage in good professional practice. The next question addresses how this happens.

Can action research increase your autonomy as a professional?

Teacher autonomy, linked to improvements in practice, can be a feature in action research. Action research offers teacher-researchers opportunities to become respected as academic knowers in the education field.

My action research experiences with pupils with language difficulties led me to question the assumptions in the literature in the field. It caused me to probe previous assumptions in my own thinking. I believe that the progression in my autonomy matched the progression in my practice.

Can action research help me contribute to the knowledge base of the teaching profession?

This form of action research allows you as a teacher to illuminate your classroom so that the educational community can view it. The authenticity of this form of action research allows you to experience Dewey's (1897) perception that education is a social process; it is not a preparation for life. It is life itself. Elliott (1991) says that action research can make educational practice more reflective. Here are some quotations from the authors of this book, written during their research, which give a flavour of how this methodology can add to professional practice:

> My research could add to school practice or policy decisions in the areas of language difficulties.
>
> I want involvement with the whole learning community.

Teaching is about asking questions and questioning answers.

Teaching and learning involves scrutinising practice and interrogating one's values so as to improve what one is doing.

Sharing learning through experience.

Improving practice leads to sustainable benefits for pupils and teacher.

McNiff says that this action research methodology allows me, the teacher-researcher, to 'be reflective of my own practice in order to enhance the quality of education for my pupils and myself' (1988: 1). Researching in this methodology is still suitable for all teachers who wish to develop professionally by doing research projects on issues of current practical relevance to them so as to improve their knowledge and practice.

The research reports you write will include classroom research vignettes. The vignettes that I have described added to my, and others', professional understanding and knowledge in the following ways:

- I was researching issues of total relevance to my work life.
- I analysed, judged, formulated solutions, compiled data and shared it with my school community.
- I presented what I had learned to others and published it in ways that invited others to consider it as part of their self-assessment toolkit.
- I did so in a way that is based on the life values that I hold dearest.

The criteria on which my claims to new knowledge will be judged are these very values and the following chapter will explain this process.

Reflective activity

- Consider the theory–practice divide and name any traditional theory of teaching and learning that has relevance for your teaching and/or your students' learning.
- Think of a metaphor for how you position theory in your practice.
- Represent this visually or write about it.

I have told you of my journey to select an action research methodology. My final choice resonates with the explanation of self-study and living theory action research approaches of Whitehead and McNiff (2006). My research methodology is a personal, practical, context-driven, collaborative research approach that allows me to investigate my practice.

Many have tried to box action research into a format that suits a transmission model for institutional use. Some have argued that this form of free flowing research is more about methods than a methodology that is practical rather than philosophically based. I would disagree with this because the form of action research in this book is firmly underpinned by a philosophy that is grounded in the values that researchers hold, in life experiences and has been tested successfully at the highest level of scholarship (see PhD awards on <http://www.eari.ie>, <http://www.jeanmcniff.com>, <http://www.actionresearch.net> among others).

Chapter summary

This chapter has introduced you to empirical, interpretive and action research paradigms and their importance in classroom research and for professional development. I showed how to question the relevance of each paradigm for your research settings so as to help you select your methodology. The world view that underpins a research methodology was questioned by asking 'Where am I placed as a professional within the paradigm?' The relationship between this world view and how you conduct your research was queried by asking 'Does it allow me to think professionally, act and reflect on my practice?' Research methodology and professional development were linked by examining how the underpinning values of the paradigm can increase one's autonomy as a professional. Finally we considered how the writing of your research report can potentially contribute to the knowledge base of the teaching profession.

The final chapters of this book show how classroom research to enhance practice and professional development is a legitimate and rigorous form of research. It is grounded in standards of judgement that, in addition to the traditional standards, test claims at personal, social and wider community levels.

Further reading

Carr, W. and Kemmis, S. (1986) *Becoming Critical: Education, Knowledge and Action Research*, London: Falmer Press.
Gives a classic overview. In addition to discussions on teachers, researchers and curriculum, it introduces readers to a critical approach to the theory and practice dilemmas for educational research, reform and the role of the profession.

Cohen, L., Manion, L. and Morrison, K. (2007) *Research Methods in Education*, 6th edn, London: RoutledgeFalmer.
Provides an extensive repertoire of research methods, all of which are well explained. This is a magnificent toolkit and useful for all forms of educational research, but you would need to query if its shiny tools are appropriate for your research, its context, values and methodology.

Hitchcock, G. and Hughes, D. (1995) *Research and the Teacher*, 2nd edn, London: Routledge, 1995.
Focuses on rigorous and practical school-based research and raises issues around the links between the teacher, teaching, research and reflection. Although it could be considered dated, it provides definitions for teachers of research methodologies from scientific to action research.

Lather, P. (2006) 'Paradigm Proliferation as a Good Thing to Think With: Teaching Research in Education as a Wild Profusion', *International Journal of Qualitative Studies in Education*, 19(1), January–February, 35–57.

A seminal article, which challenges paradigm debates. Lather proposes that methodologies should be investigated by the educational researcher having regard to ideas around objectivity, complicity, difference, interpretation and legitimisation.

Part 4

Generating evidence from data
Making meaning

Bernie Sullivan

In this part we introduce you to the final phases in an action research project. In the previous chapters, we discussed how to engage with the various stages in the development of an action plan. This included the identification of your educational values, critical reflection on your practice, choosing a methodology to suit your purpose and the collection of your data. This part shows how you can draw together the various strands of the research as you articulate the findings from your research project. At this stage of the process the main concern is with meaning-making, in the course of which you attempt to develop an enhanced understanding of your practice through the use of the skills of self-reflection and self-evaluation. Hamilton and Pinnegar suggest that 'understanding the self is an essential aspect for generating change and developing new knowledge' (1998: 241). The learning emanating from the process of self-reflection represents new knowledge, which has the potential to result in the development of a theory of practice.

In Chapter 7 I engage with the process of providing evidence to demonstrate that improvement has taken place in your practice or that your understanding of your practice has been enhanced. I indicate how the various pieces of data that have been gathered in the course of carrying out the research can be analysed as you seek evidence of any improvements and increased understanding. I use an example from my own practice to illustrate the process of turning data into evidence. Central to this process is the part played by your values in the research, in particular the extent to which you have managed to achieve the realisation of these values in your practice. Establishing a link between your values and the outcomes of the research can be an important element in the process of providing evidence to support your claim to have achieved improvement in your practice.

Chapter 8 demonstrates how you can develop a theory of practice by providing descriptions and explanations of your practice (Whitehead and McNiff 2006). This process occurs as you attempt to make sense of your research findings, in the course of which new knowledge about your practice emerges. The research findings may confirm your expectations about your research; equally, there may emerge unexpected or surprising results from the research. The new knowledge can be considered unique in the sense that it will have emerged from your self-reflection on your practice, and thus constitutes what Polanyi (1958) refers to as personal knowledge. While you may incorporate established theories in the literature into your research, it is important to adopt a critical stance towards such abstract theories, indicating where they differ from the new knowledge you have generated. This critical approach will help to strengthen the validity of your personal theory of practice, which is a potential outcome of your research. In this chapter, I will indicate how to articulate the significance of your research for yourself and others, and outline the importance of disseminating the findings from your research.

Chapter 7

Providing evidence of improved practice

This chapter explores:

- how to collate and analyse your data
- how to provide evidence of improvement in your practice, in your understanding of your practice or in your thinking processes
- how to establish a link between improvements achieved and your values.

Introduction

In the preceding chapters we provided guidelines on how to identify an area of concern to you in your practice where you feel there is room for improvement, how to articulate the values that cause you to be concerned, how to critically reflect on your practice in order to achieve greater understanding of the reasons for your concerns, how to develop an action plan aimed at addressing your concerns and how to implement that plan, including how to systematically gather data in the course of carrying out your plan. In this chapter the project will be taken a stage further, and we introduce you to the process of analysing your data and using it to provide evidence of any improvement that you may have achieved in your practice or in your understanding of your practice. Apple seems to expect that all teachers should have an automatic involvement in trying to improve their practices when he states, 'All educators (one would hope) are deeply committed to making schools better places to be' (1996: 107).

As you engage with the cycles of action and reflection that are consistent with an action research approach, you will more than likely accumulate a considerable amount of data relating to your project, including:

- entries in your reflective journal
- informal notes written at the end of a teaching session
- comments from your students

- results of tests administered to students
- critical feedback from teaching colleagues or critical friends
- audiotapes, video recordings, photographs or film clips.

All of these sources of data combine to form your data archive and will be of immense value in providing evidence to support your claim to have improved your practice. Of particular benefit are the critical comments of colleagues, as these observations can be used in the process of triangulation. Triangulation provides the researcher with the opportunity of having the findings of the research corroborated by others not directly involved in the research, and can add to the validity of the research and the reliability of the outcomes. Robson (1993) regards triangulation as an indispensable tool in research, and claims that it improves the quality of the data and the accuracy of the findings. Cohen, Manion and Morrison describe triangulation as 'a powerful way of demonstrating concurrent validity' (2007: 141).

As you sift through the various pieces of data and look for examples to identify where you may have achieved improvement, you are engaging in the process of analysing your data. You may wish to take the option of analysing your data as you collect it, rather than waiting until the conclusion of your research. This approach is certainly to be recommended in the case of audio and video tapes, the transcription of which can be time-consuming. However, further analysis of your data will be required when you have completed your research, as it is only then that you will have a clear picture of the whole process. Through this final, in-depth analysis of your data you may come to the conclusion that an improvement in a particular area of your practice has occurred, or that you have achieved an enhanced understanding of your practice.

The process of analysing your data may not be easy or straightforward, particularly if you adopt a rigorous and thorough stance in your self-reflection. Such rigour could expose any shortcomings or weaknesses in your practice, leaving you with feelings of vulnerability. Cook outlines some of the difficulties that can occur during the course of the data analysis when she writes:

> It is difficult for those who are embedded in their work (and workplace stories) to take themselves from the descriptive mode to the analytical, especially when an immediate consequence of such dialectical engagement can be that participants are left open to feelings of confusion, doubt and uncertainty rather than enlightenment.

(Cook 2009: 285)

In a similar vein, Pithouse, Mitchell and Weber (2009), drawing on the ideas of Dadds (1993), suggest that 'when the "self" we come to see in self-study is not the "self" we think we are, or the "self" we would like to be' (2009: 47), it makes us feel uncomfortable. Nevertheless, if you can overcome any sense of reluctance and apprehension as you engage in honest and critical reflection on your data, you will be well rewarded as your understanding of your practice and desire to improve it will be enhanced.

In the process of analysing your data, you will need to return to your initial action plan in order to determine to what extent you have been successful in achieving the stated aims of your research project. You will also need to revisit the values that you have identified as being fundamental to your work, in order to establish whether you are living out these values in your practice. An examination of your data archive may reveal data that demonstrates that you have achieved your aim or that you are living to your values. This data can provide evidence to support your claim to have improved your practice or your understanding of your practice. Alternatively, the data could indicate that there has not been any significant improvement in your practice, but this discovery in itself represents at the very least an increase in self-knowledge and self-awareness, thus constituting new knowledge of your practice. It is important also to have an awareness of the possibility that there may be unintended outcomes of your research, in addition to those you had planned for or more or less expected, and that these can be equally valid to the research process. Kemmis and McTaggart suggest that the action researcher's reflection on practice should include the questions: 'What are the intended and unintended effects?' and 'What caused these effects?' (1988: 88).

It may be helpful to ask yourself some questions as you seek evidence of improvement in your practice, and the following reflective activity may be useful in this regard.

Reflective activity

Having reflected on your practice, ask yourself:

- Can I identify any area where there has been an improvement?
- Can I show evidence of this improvement in practice?
- Can I establish a link between the improvement and my values?
- Can I document the process of change that led to the improvement?
- Do colleagues or critical friends agree there has been an improvement in my practice?
- Can I show there has been an improvement in my understanding of my practice?
- Does my reflection on my practice indicate an enhancement in my thinking processes?

As you reflect on these or similar questions, you may find that the evidence you require is readily available, especially if you have been documenting aspects of your research regularly in your reflective journal. Later on in this chapter I will return to the above questions and discuss them in relation to the following example from my research, as I analyse the data collected during the course of the research and indicate where I can point to evidence of improvement in my practice.

Example from my research

To illustrate the process of showing evidence of improvement in practice, I will narrate an incident from my own research, which occurred when I was carrying out a small-scale research project for a module of my MA course. In keeping with the principles of the action research approach that I had chosen for my methodology, I began to reflect on my practice with a view to uncovering an area in which I might be able to effect improvement. My reflection led to the realisation that there was one aspect of my practice that was causing me disquiet. This dissonance that I experienced in my teaching practice related to a child in my class, for whom I shall use the pseudonym Caroline.

Narrative of my research

Caroline was an 11-year-old girl, in her final year of primary school. She had a history of non-completion of homework and a related non-attendance problem. The non-attendance issue arose in the following manner. After several incidences of Caroline arriving in school with homework either not done at all or not finished, in spite of specific requests to her to complete her homework, I eventually said that she would have to do the homework in detention the following day. However, Caroline did not come to school the following day, or for a number of days thereafter, thus adding the problem of non-attendance to the no-homework issue.

When you consider the above situation you may be inclined towards a view, as I was initially, that I had no responsibility for the unsatisfactory state of affairs, and that Caroline may have caused the problem by virtue of her actions in not doing her homework and not coming to school. You may agree with my contention that Caroline had been given ample opportunity to comply with her homework requirements, a necessity if she was to be able to keep up with her work in class and be adequately prepared for the challenges of second level schooling the following year. You may also feel that I was justified in my stance that if she were not reprimanded for not doing her homework, the rest of the class would begin taking the same liberties. At that time, my understanding of the concept of equality was such that I felt obliged to treat all pupils the same, and the idea of making concessions to any pupil was anathema to my value of fairness.

At a later stage in my research undertakings, my reflection on these issues led to a change in my thinking that enabled me to develop a more enlightened and more socially-just understanding of equality (Sullivan 2006). My enhanced thinking on the subject resulted in making a distinction between equality and sameness, and in realising that treating children equally did not necessarily mean treating them all the same, but rather taking account of their differences. I began, therefore, to practise 'a politics that recognises rather than represses difference' (Young 1990: 10).

Nevertheless, in spite of my sense of justification in relation to the stance I had taken, I continued to reflect on the matter. You will realise the importance of continuous reflection on your actions as you read of the ideas that emerged from my further reflection.

Narrative of my research continues

When I reflected on my classroom situation, as required by my action research methodology, I came to realise that, while Caroline may indeed have initiated the unsatisfactory state of affairs through her consistent failure to complete her homework, I had to take some responsibility for her continuing absence from school. Through my action in giving her detention I had, however unwittingly, contributed to the situation that led her to absent herself from school. I recalled Hartog's thoughts on a similar incident, when she said, 'entering into the anxiety, pain, fear, despair and hatred that another sentient human being experiences as a result of your actions' (2004: 310) is disturbing.

Looking at the situation from Caroline's point of view, I felt that it would be very difficult for her to extricate herself from her difficult circumstances with any degree of confidence or self-worth. It would be incumbent on me, therefore, as the adult in the situation, to find a solution that did not result in a loss of face for Caroline. The realisation that I had some responsibility for what had occurred came as a shock to me, but it also represented significant learning for me around the necessity for having greater accountability for my actions, as well as greater awareness of the effect that my actions could have on a powerless, voiceless pupil. Further reflection on the issue engendered in me a deep commitment towards finding a solution to the problem and to ending the cycle of no homework, leading to absence, in which Caroline was now enmeshed.

You can see from the above narrative how critical reflection often leads to a plan of action. I began to investigate my reasons for wishing to take action and came to the conclusion that my sense of unease and dissatisfaction with my situation was caused by the fact that my educational values were not being realised in my practice. As a result, I was experiencing myself as a living contradiction (Whitehead 1989), a concept that we have discussed in Chapter 4. These are some of my educational values:

- equality – all pupils treated equally within the educational system
- lifelong learning – all pupils remaining in the educational system for as long as possible

- democratic principles in education, to give educators greater autonomy in their classrooms, and ensure that pupils have a voice in the educational system
- a strong work ethic and regular school attendance, which is vital for success in education
- social justice as a means of achieving equal rights for all pupils in education.

When you have identified your personal educational values, as we have outlined in previous chapters, you will feel a sense of commitment to living to those values, and any action plan you may formulate will help you to do this. When addressing the situation with Caroline, I hoped that my values around lifelong learning, a strong work ethic and regular school attendance would enable me to help her to reach her full educational potential. I was concerned that someone who could absent herself from school as easily as Caroline had just done would eventually feature among the statistics of early school-leavers, dropping out of the educational system as soon as she could legally do so. I began to formulate an action plan that I hoped would encourage her to greater participation in the educational system and give her the confidence and self-belief to develop a commitment to lifelong education.

Action plan

The first step in my action research plan was to talk to Caroline and endeavour to find out why she was having difficulty in completing her homework. You can see from this approach that I was fulfilling my value around the importance of enabling pupils to have a voice in decisions on educational matters concerning them. Freire highlights the inhumanity inherent in the denial of voice to others when he says, 'to alienate men [sic] from their own decision-making is to change them into objects' (1972: 73). My action research plan also provided an opportunity for the practice of the democratic principles in education to which I was committed, and that I have listed among my values above.

The immediate problem that confronted me was how I was going to get Caroline back in to school so I could begin my new approach with her. I decided to enlist the help of the school principal, who was aware of my concerns about Caroline. We agreed that if Caroline failed to turn up for school the following morning, the principal would go to her home and try to persuade her to come to school. This scenario went according to plan, and when Caroline arrived in class a little late I refrained from making any comment. I did not mention the subject of homework to Caroline that day and decided it would be better to wait until she had developed a more positive attitude towards school before embarking on my new plan with her. You can see, therefore, the importance of certain factors, such as timing and the co-operation of others, to the implementation of your action plan.

Narrative of my research continues

When Caroline seemed to be sufficiently comfortable with being back at school, I asked her why homework was causing such difficulty for her. She explained that her mother went to work as soon as she arrived home from school, her older siblings were either at work or at second level schools, and there was nobody to help her with homework, or even to ask if she had completed it. I asked if there were particular areas of homework that were proving more difficult than others for her, and she answered that she found it hard to cope with mathematics homework. I was aware from her homework that mathematics could be problematic for her. I proposed, therefore, that she should just do her English homework for the moment and omit doing her mathematics homework. Caroline seemed happy with this arrangement.

The following day Caroline arrived in school, having completed the English homework. We continued with this programme of action for the rest of the week, with Caroline doing her reduced homework and in attendance every day. At the end of the week, I noted in my reflective journal that school had been less stressful for me, that Caroline looked happier and more relaxed, and that I felt there was less tension in our relationship since I had consulted with Caroline about the homework issue.

After two weeks I decided that it was time to review the situation, in line with the cycles of reflection and action that characterise an action research methodology. I had noted in my research journal that Caroline's learning support teacher had remarked to me that she seemed more interested in her work lately and that her attendance had improved. I felt, therefore, that it was appropriate to begin another cycle of my research project. I had a conversation with Caroline in which I asked how she felt she was getting on with her homework. She said she was finding it much easier and that she liked school now. I asked her if she would be willing to attempt her mathematics homework. I explained to her that it did not matter if she got it wrong, but that it would be important for her to make an attempt at doing it so that she would be able to cope with this subject when she moved on to second level school. I suggested that if she was going to attempt the mathematics homework, she need only do half of her English homework. She replied that she would attempt the mathematics and do all the English homework!

Caroline was as good as her word and on the following day produced a reasonable effort at the mathematics homework, as well as completing all her English homework. She continued with this course of action for the rest of her time in primary school. I had now finished my action research project and needed to write up my report. I wrote to Caroline's mother to ask her for permission to document the course of action I had undertaken with her, promising not to reveal her identify, in keeping with the terms of my ethical statement. Caroline's mother gave her consent.

Analysis of data

Analysing your data is an essential element of your action research project. It requires that you subject your data to detailed scrutiny as you seek to interpret your actions and produce explanations for them. It involves examining the aims of your research to determine to what extent you have achieved them, and looking at your values to ascertain whether you have succeeded in living up to them. As you begin to make sense of your data you will learn how to use the findings of your research to demonstrate the improvements you have achieved. To help you to understand how to analyse your data I will describe the process with reference to the example from my practice that I outlined above.

I had documented the above vignette, and my reflections on it, in my reflective journal. I had kept a record of Caroline's school attendance and her homework. I had noted any comments on Caroline from a teaching colleague. The school principal had recorded her observations of how I had tried a new approach with Caroline and her thoughts on how the matter had progressed, and she had made her account of events available to me. I had also retained the letter from Caroline's mother, details of conversations between Caroline and me, and Caroline's thoughts at the end of the project on how she felt following my change in approach. The documents that I have listed here all formed part of my research archive, which I could now use as I searched for evidence of improvement in my teaching practice, with particular emphasis on my new approach to solving the difficulties that I had been experiencing with Caroline.

Reflective activity

When you get to the stage of analysing your data, you may find it helpful to focus again on the main elements of your research project. Asking yourself the following questions will help you achieve this focus:

- What are the aims of my research?
- What are my values?
- Have I recorded my reflections on my research in my journal?
- What sources of data can I produce?
- Have I obtained written comments from colleagues?

The information that you gather through answering these questions will help to clarify issues as you analyse your data. When you reflect on your answers you will have a clearer picture of what you have achieved through doing your research. In the next few paragraphs I will outline my learning through my reflections.

Reflections on actions

It is evident from the vignette presented in this chapter that I had brought about a change in my practice. I needed, therefore, to examine whether that change could be construed as an improvement in my practice. As a first step, I decided to reflect critically on the situation as it was before I had introduced my change in approach. While accepting that ground rules are needed in a classroom, including rules relating to homework, I now questioned whether they needed to be enforced so rigidly and so uniformly. I came to the conclusion that a more relaxed and flexible approach might work better with some pupils, in which case a change of approach was certainly worth a try. This conclusion represented a change in my thinking, signalling a move from a rather dogmatic, authoritarian stance to one of greater fluidity and variability. This was an improvement in my thinking that now needed to be replicated in my practice.

When it became apparent through my reflection on the matter that a new approach in my practice was needed, I came up with a new action plan: to ask Caroline about her difficulties with homework. In so doing, I was living out in my practice my value of adopting a democratic approach to education that would enable pupils to have a voice in educational decisions affecting them. Davies talks about 'the effectiveness of involving pupils in educational decision-making' (Davies 2001, cited in Ruddock and McIntyre, 2007: 5). Similarly, Devine (2004) argues that adults should provide children with the opportunity to voice their opinion on matters directly of concern to them. The change in my approach was innovative as it would not have been the norm for me previously to consult pupils about their homework. In agreement with Freire (1972), I now recognised the importance of talking to students to achieve a more emancipatory approach to teaching and learning.

My action in consulting Caroline represented a new approach in my understanding of pupil–teacher relationships. Previously I would have seen such relationships as being necessarily unequal, with the teacher or adult having the more powerful role in decision making and the pupil having a lesser, more subordinate role. However, when I spoke to Caroline on her return to school, we were beginning a process of creating a more equal relationship. When I suggested that she might do a reduced amount of homework, she readily agreed and fulfilled her part of the contract by completing the homework. It appeared that being consulted on the matter acted as an impetus to get her homework back on track. The new, more equal relationship continued as we negotiated her return to doing her mathematics homework. The change in relationship between us could be described in the light of Buber's (1958) ideas on this topic. Buber differentiated between an 'I–it' relationship, where one person dominates and sees the other as an object, rather than as another human being of equal value, and an 'I–thou' relationship, in which each person sees the other as an equal, deserving of the utmost respect and consideration. My new approach to Caroline reflected characteristics of an 'I–thou' relationship, in contrast to our previous 'I–it' relationship, and consequently could be described as an improvement on the former position.

In trying to get Caroline to comply with homework regulations, I was attempting to get her to behave in the same way as all the other pupils. In other words, I viewed my class more or less as a homogeneous group, all motivated to achieve high standards in their work. Consistent with this view, I had high expectations of all pupils. Conscious also of children's desire for fairness in one's dealings with them, I did not think it appropriate to treat one pupil differently from the others. However, in devising my action plan for Caroline, I realised that I could only progress the situation by treating her as an individual and by having a one-to-one conversation with her. In spite of my misgivings around having to make concessions for one pupil, adopting the new approach to homework with Caroline did not appear to impact negatively on the rest of the class, who continued to work as they always had. Consequently, in agreement with Schön (1983), I believe that each student makes up a universe of one, whose potential, problems and pace of work must be appreciated as the teacher reflects-in-action on the design of her work.

One of my concerns about Caroline's failure to complete her homework was the possibility that she might fall behind in her work. This would have implications for her ability to negotiate the curriculum successfully at second level school and could give her an excuse for dropping out of school early. My thinking around this topic changed somewhat when I allowed Caroline to complete part of her homework, instead of having to do the whole lot, as I realised that it would be an improvement if she did part of the homework rather than none of it. My reflection on this situation led me to understand that an over-emphasis on completing the curriculum could put pupils under undue pressure, leaving them with a negative view of the learning process and of schooling in general. I came to the realisation that, in the area of curriculum, quality was of more importance than quantity, and that it was unrealistic to expect that all pupils would cover the entire curriculum. I needed, therefore, to adopt a more critical stance towards curriculum and to realise, like Stenhouse (1975), that teachers must be critics of work in the curriculum, not docile agents.

The impetus that inspired my research project from the beginning was my concern for Caroline, and this concern was sustained throughout the research. I was concerned that she was not working to the best of her ability, that she would not be able to survive academically at second level school, and that she could be at risk of dropping out of the educational system early as a result of her inability to cope with the workload involved. When I reflected on my concerns and my reasons for them, I realised that they arose out of my sense of caring for Caroline. However, while I may have had an awareness of this sense of care at an early stage in the research, I do not think it was obvious to Caroline until I brought about changes in my practice, such as consulting her and involving her in decision making about her homework. Those changes were reflected in our changed relationship, which could now be described as a caring one. In agreement with Noddings (1992), I came to the realisation that no genuine improvement is possible without placing care at the centre of experience for teachers and pupils.

Evidence of improvement in practice and understanding of practice

I now return to the questions that I outlined at the beginning of this chapter and will address these questions in the context of the example from my research, and in accordance with the analysis of my data from this research. In answer to the first question, 'Can I identify any area of my practice where there has been an improvement?', I suggest that my change in approach to solving the difficulties I was encountering with Caroline constitutes an improvement to my practice. It reflects an improvement in the sense that my new, more accommodating approach produced better outcomes than my previous more rigid method had done. These outcomes were better because they represented a more positive outlook for Caroline and had the potential to increase her participation in the educational system.

In reply to the second question, 'Can I show evidence of the improvement in my practice?', I can point to two such instances in my practice, which I have described in the example from my research. The first occurred when Caroline began to attend school more regularly, and the second when she got back on track with her homework. These two events signified a considerable improvement on the situation that existed before my intervention through my action research project, when Caroline's education was at serious risk because of her reluctance to complete her homework and her long absences from school.

In response to the question 'Can I establish a link between the improvement in practice and my values?', I reply that I can make a connection with three of the values that I identified earlier in this chapter: my commitments to lifelong learning, democratic principles in education and regular school attendance. In changing my approach for the purpose of getting Caroline back to school, I was providing her with the opportunity for long-term participation in the educational system. In taking action to change my practice I was making a democratic decision about my work, and in consulting Caroline about completing her homework, I was ensuring that she had a voice in matters concerning her education. Through getting Caroline back to school and sorting out the homework problem, I was fulfilling my values around regular attendance and a strong work ethic. You can perceive, therefore, the importance of establishing a link between any improvement in your practice and the values that underpin your practice.

The fourth question was 'Can I document the process of change that led to the improvement?' The process of change began with my reflection on my practice with a view to finding a solution to what I perceived to be an unsatisfactory situation concerning Caroline. The process continued with the realisation that I had within my power the capacity to effect change. The change in my thinking was followed by the development of a new action plan. When this plan was implemented, it brought about the desired change, which, as I have previously explained, represented a considerable improvement on the original situation.

In answering the next question, 'Do colleagues or critical friends agree that improvement has taken place?', I wish to refer to the items that I mentioned as being stored in my data archive, which included comments from a colleague and the school principal, and the letter I had received from Caroline's mother at the end of the project. My colleague, who had provided learning support in mathematics for Caroline, had written:

> Her attendance was very erratic – missing a day or two every week. Then she was absent for quite a long spell. It was frustrating, knowing the difficulty she would have in catching up. Eventually, Caroline returned and as time progressed her attendance was excellent. She began to take an interest in her work.

This extract from my colleague's notes indicates the previous unsatisfactory situation regarding Caroline's attendance and then the improvement, in her attendance and her work, following my intervention. The school principal states explicitly that she feels the improvement in Caroline's situation is a direct result of my plan of action, when she says:

> From my vantage point, this strategy must be working. When I ask Caroline's teacher about homework, I am told there is no problem. Caroline herself looks brighter, has shown initiative on a few occasions and seems to like getting responsibilities.

At the end of my research project I wrote to Caroline's mother to ask for her permission to write a report on the project, in accordance with my ethical statement. In a letter granting permission, she included the following observations:

> I am very pleased with her improvement both at home and in school, and the fact that all her mystery illnesses have disappeared, which proves she is happier with her lot. Whatever approach you used certainly worked.

The three individuals whose views are quoted here, and who served as a validation group for my research findings, are all in agreement that improvement has taken place. Their comments can be considered as providing triangulation, since they corroborate the findings of my research. You will have gathered from this, therefore, the importance of having data from observers not directly involved in the research project in order to add to the validity of your research.

The penultimate question was 'Can I show that there has been improvement in my understanding of my practice?' Originally, my practice appeared to be rather rigid and inflexible, a situation with which I was not entirely comfortable, but nevertheless I considered to be unavoidable in the interests of treating all pupils equally and attempting to ensure that all pupils covered the whole curriculum. However, when I developed my new action plan, my understanding of my practice changed to the extent that I realised that I could treat some children differently, which would not violate my commitment to equality, and that I did not have to adhere slavishly to the prescribed curriculum but could adapt it to suit the needs of individual pupils. Like Stenhouse (1975), I became aware of the benefits of adopting a process-based model of curriculum, rather than a product-based model.

The final question was 'Does my reflection on my practice indicate an enhancement in my thinking processes?' My reflection on my practice led first to a change in my thinking, before the changes that took place in my practice. The change in my thinking occurred when I realised I had some responsibility for Caroline's situation, and therefore there was an onus on me to try to remedy it. There was also a change in my thinking when I decided to consult Caroline about her homework, as this decision meant that I was now treating her as a person with an important contribution to make towards solving the problem, rather than as an inferior pupil, which is the perception that my previous attitude towards her may have indicated. This changed relationship is a reflection of the democratic approach to education recommended by Dewey (1966), who described such an approach as the participation or sharing in an activity where the teacher is a learner and the learner is, without knowing it, a teacher. I suggest that these changes to my thinking represented an improvement on my previous thinking, and could thus be considered to have enhanced my thinking processes.

Chapter summary

In this chapter you have been introduced to the process of conducting an in-depth analysis of the data collected in a practice-based research project. You have been made aware of the importance of systematically gathering your data and storing it in a data archive, where it will be readily available when you need it to provide evidence for the findings of your research. The reflective journal that you have been keeping since the beginning of your research will also be a source of data. You have learned how you can relate the findings of your research to your values, and show whether or not you have succeeded in living according to these values in your practice. The list of questions that I provided at the beginning of this chapter can be helpful in the task of critically reflecting on your research project, and in identifying areas of improvement in your practice and understanding of your practice. The concept of triangulation has been explained as a process that can add rigour and robustness to the validity of your research through providing corroborating evidence from other reliable sources. Finally, you have learned that the improvement you achieve through carrying out your research can be an improvement in your practice, your understanding of your practice, or your thinking processes. These improvements constitute new knowledge and contain the potential to develop into a theory of practice. I will discuss this process in the next chapter.

Further reading

Freire, P. (1972) *Pedagogy of the Oppressed*, London: Sheed and Ward.
    Describes the lack of respect shown to learners when they are subjected to a transmission
    model of education rather than a liberating co-operative approach.
Noddings, N. (1992) *The Challenge to Care in Schools: An Alternative Approach to Educa-
    tion*, New York: Teachers College.
    Promotes the idea of having an ethic of care towards pupils.
Schön, D. (1983) *The Reflective Practitioner: How Professionals Think in Action*, New
    York: Basic Books.
    An introduction to the idea of constant self-reflection as a means towards improvement.
Whitehead, J. (1989) 'Creating a Living Educational Theory from Questions of the Kind,
    "How do I Improve my Practice?"', *Cambridge Journal of Education*, 19(1), 41–52,
    available online at <http://www.actionresearch.net/writings/livtheory.html> (accessed
    25 May 2011).
    A good guide to the process of developing a personal theory of one's practice.

Chapter 8

Developing theory from practice

This chapter explores:

- how to document the learning from your research project
- how your new knowledge can develop into a theory of practice
- the significance of your findings for yourself and others
- the importance of sustaining improvement in your practice.

Introduction

The main thrust of this chapter is to indicate how the findings from your research, which you have uncovered through a detailed analysis of your data and the resulting evidence you have produced, can be used in the development of a theory of your practice. In the course of articulating your findings, you may have come to an understanding that your research has significance at various levels – for yourself at a personal level, for your pupils at the micro level of your school, and for the wider community at the macro level of educational practice in general. It is important to be aware of the significance of your research and to try to find ways to ensure that others also learn of its significance. You might, therefore, investigate methods of disseminating the findings of your research so that others can benefit from your experience, and may be encouraged to undertake similar research projects that could result in an enhancement in their educational practices. In this manner, your research findings could have far-reaching effects and in the process you could have an influence on social formations, which Whitehead (2004) considers to be one of the outcomes of living theory action research.

To help you to come to a deeper understanding of the significance of your research and the benefits of disseminating the findings from your research, you might ask yourself the following questions as you reflect on your research project. Focusing on these questions will assist you in developing an awareness of the importance of your research and ensuring the sustainability of your commitment to improvement in your practice. It may also help you to understand how you could influence other practitioners to engage in similar research projects.

Reflective activity

Ask yourself:

- What have I learned from engaging in my research?
- How will my learning from this project inform my future practice?
- How have my pupils benefited from the research project?
- Can I show the significance of my research for others, besides myself and my pupils?
- How can I share my new knowledge with other colleagues?
- How can I influence others to undertake similar research projects leading to improvement in their practices?
- What measures can I put in place to ensure the sustainability of the improvement in my own practice?

In traditional forms of educational research the teacher was not usually regarded as a knowledge-creating researcher. While the teacher may have participated in the research to the extent of observing pupils, filling in or distributing questionnaires, gathering data, giving feedback and corroborating the findings of the researcher, developing theories from the research findings was not considered to be the teacher's role; this was the role of the academic researcher. To use Schön's (1983) terminology, the academic researcher worked in the high ground of theory while the teacher toiled in the swampy lowland of practice. Gewirtz et al. (2009) argue that although teachers are considered to be professionals, very often they have no power to influence policy. They also claim that as a consequence of the 'raising standards' agenda, 'teachers have been reconfigured as technicians rather than as intellectuals in their own right' (2009: 569). However, in a self-study action research methodology, which recognises the role of teacher-as-researcher (Stenhouse, 1975), teachers are viewed as researchers in their own right, eminently capable of developing theories from their educational practices. In this context Somekh (2010), quoting Elliott (1976), states that changes in practice as a result of 'self-monitoring' were evidence of theorising. O'Hanlon too is of the view that researchers can 'define their own forms of valid knowledge, and present them as educational theories' (2002: 117). This broader view of research could overcome the dichotomous theory–practice divide that often acts as a barrier to teachers who wish to have autonomy over their research projects. It could also contribute to dissipating the effects of the unequal power relations embedded in such artificially created constructs.

In Chapter 7, you were introduced to the process of analysing data and using it to provide evidence of improvement in your practice or your understanding of your practice. As explained in that chapter, there may not necessarily be any significant improvement in your practice but this discovery in itself constitutes an enhancement in your understanding of your practice and can be considered new learning for you. The learning resulting from the process of analysing your data represents new knowledge and can be used to develop a theory of your practice. The new knowledge may be something that you have discovered about your own learning. It could also be something that you knew at an implicit level previously, in what Polanyi (1958) refers to as tacit knowledge, but have now come to articulate in a more explicit manner as a result of engaging in your research project. In either case, the new knowledge will have emerged through continuous reflection in accordance with the action research cycles with which you engaged during your research project.

The process of developing a theory of practice from your research project is not easy and often occurs only after you have engaged in a series of positive actions and critical reflections. It requires great clarity in setting out the aims and objectives of your research and a clear focus on your research question. This is not always a straightforward or linear process. You may have to change direction and begin a new cycle of action research on more than one occasion as you attempt to engage with the problems that become apparent as you negotiate your way through the action research project and reflect on the research process. McNiff (2002) depicts this process as a series of spirals developing in a generative transformational process from the original action research cycles of planning, acting and reflecting. You need to collect data consistently and systematically, right from the beginning of your research. Your data analysis needs to be rigorous and methodical, in order to gain optimum insight into the progress of your research and to indicate where, when, why and how improvement has taken place in your practice. If you enlist the support of a group of critical teaching colleagues when you begin your research, they may provide invaluable corroborative data as you seek evidence to establish firmly the grounds for your claim to knowledge through the process known as triangulation. By demonstrating that you have endeavoured to fulfil your ontological and epistemological values you will have further evidence of your claim to have created new knowledge. Your claim to knowledge, which arises from your new learning around your educational practice, represents your personal theory of your practice.

If you are submitting a written account of your research to an educational institution for the purpose of having it accredited, the institution will probably have its own assessment criteria, which you will need to show that you have met in the course of carrying out your research. Your research supervisor will guide you in this matter. In traditional forms of research the criteria are often to do with the transferability and replicability of the research findings, and these criteria can usually be met by the use of statistical data or by providing scientific proof in support of a theory. An action research approach views each research project as unique and individual; therefore, these traditional positivist criteria would not be appropriate as assessment tools for your research. As an action research methodology is values-based, the relevant values can be used to judge the quality of the research. In their living theory approach to action research, Whitehead and McNiff (2006) suggest that standards of judgement based on the researcher's ontological and epistemological values can replace the traditional criteria used in other research approaches. You may, therefore, articulate the standards of judgement that you wish to be used in assessing your research project through identifying the values that underpin your research and using them to formulate the standards of judgement.

Example from my research

I will give a brief account of an action research project that I undertook as part of my MA studies (Sullivan 2000), in order to demonstrate how you can develop a theory of practice from your research. The aim of my research was to help my pupils to make more effective use of their time in school. At the time I taught a mainstream class of 10-year-old girls in their penultimate year at primary school. I was concerned that the time-wasting in which they often engaged could have a detrimental effect on the quality of education they received and, ultimately, on their future opportunities in life. My concerns arose when I realised that a lot of time was being spent on non-learning activities and could thus be regarded as time wasted. This situation was in direct opposition to my epistemology of education at that time, which was premised on the view that pupils' interests in school were best served by a specific focus on teaching and learning. Consequently, the time-wasting activities in which my pupils engaged seemed to me to be counter-productive, as I subscribe to Fisher's (1995) view that maximum use should be made of classroom learning time. Among the time-wasting activities that I had in mind were:

- latecomers strolling in, thus delaying the start of class
- leaving homework at home, necessitating discussion of the issue
- not taking home the textbook required for a homework assignment
- having arguments in the school yard, requiring resolution during class time
- delays in change over from one subject to another
- being easily distracted and not giving full attention to homework.

You can see how such activities could prevent me from living according to my values around encouraging pupils to have a strong work ethic, and ensuring that my pupils received the maximum benefit from the educational system. You may also note that my values of social justice and equality were being compromised, if my pupils lost out on any teaching and learning time. Because of the time-wasting activities listed above, I was experiencing dissonance between my educational values and what was occurring daily in my classroom. I was, therefore, positioned as a 'living contradiction', as explicated by Whitehead (1989), and needed to try to resolve the situation in order to experience a greater sense of equilibrium in my classroom.

I began my action plan by consulting my pupils, and tape-recording this consultation, having received permission from the pupils' parents and the pupils themselves, in keeping with the ethical considerations on carrying out research as outlined by Hitchcock and Hughes (1995). I began the conversation by explaining to the pupils that I was concerned that they might not be making the best use of their time in school. To my surprise, they were well aware of the extent of their time-wasting, and were even able to add to my list of time-wasting activities. For example, they admitted to often asking me time-delaying questions so that I would continue with a subject that they enjoyed for a while longer, rather than moving on to the next subject, which they did not particularly like. When I suggested that we might embark on a project aimed at reducing the time-wasting activities, they agreed enthusiastically. I pointed out to them that the time saved through participating in the project could be spent on activities that they enjoyed, such as art or computer work.

Part of my learning from the action research example that I described in Chapter 7 related to the concept of perceiving my pupil, Caroline, as an equal participant in the research process, entitled to have her voice heard on educational issues that concerned her. This knowledge now informed my practice in the new project on which I was about to embark. From the beginning, I regarded my pupils as co-researchers, and to that end I supplied them with notebooks, which they could use as reflective diaries. I asked them what areas they wished to improve, and they suggested:

- coming to school on time
- doing all their homework
- not interrupting each other in class
- getting all schoolwork completed
- promptness in the changeover from one subject to another
- paying attention in class.

Conscious of the importance of acquiring feedback from others that could prove useful in the process of validating my research findings, I asked two colleagues if they would be willing to participate in my project through monitoring some of the pupils in regard to the above areas of improvement. Annabel provided learning support in mathematics to six of my pupils and Belinda took five pupils for English language support. They agreed to document the progress of their respective pupils during the course of the project.

Narrative of my research

In keeping with the democratic ethos that I tried to promote in my classroom, initially I suggested that each pupil could choose the time-wasting activity that she wished to address. At the end of each day the pupils were allocated a five-minute slot during which they could record in their reflective diaries the time-wasting activities they had chosen to work on for that particular day, noting whether or not they had achieved their aim. Some of the pupils asked me to confirm their opinions as to how they had performed, and I realised immediately that there was a flaw in my research design. In attempting to grant autonomy to my pupils in individually choosing their areas of improvement, I had overlooked the fact that it would be difficult for me to monitor the individual progress of all pupils, as there were 23 pupils participating in the research project.

In keeping with the cycles of reflection and action that characterise an action research approach (McNiff 1988), my reflection on the above problem revealed the need to review my action plan. I had a tape-recorded discussion with my pupils and we agreed that the whole class would work on one area of improvement for a few days, and then move on to another one. We put this plan into practice for the next two weeks, during which time I collected data on the number of latecomers, the numbers completing their schoolwork and homework, and the time it took to change from one subject to another. My two colleagues collected data in the same areas. In fulfilment of my promise to my pupils at the beginning of the project, they were rewarded with either a session in the computer room or an extra art class each week.

The research project appeared to be progressing satisfactorily at this stage. However, I noted in my reflective journal that I found the pace of the new strategy to be a bit slow moving, and had noticed that when the focus moved to another area of improvement, the pupils ceased to work on the previous one. It seemed that a certain momentum had been lost, so I felt it was time for another review, which resulted in our third tape-recorded conversation. Our new plan was to begin working on one area, then continue working on that area as well as taking on a second area on the following day. This process would continue by adding a new area each day until eventually we would be working on all areas at the same time. This could prove really effective and produce a significant improvement in the time-wasting activities. We began, therefore, what was to be the third and final cycle of our action research project.

During this phase of the research the pupils appeared for the most part to be self-motivated. They reminded each other of the area they were working on and reminded me to allow time for filling in their research diaries. I had the sense that the research was moving along with minimal input from me and that my pupils were now exercising a degree of control over the situation. As a result of time saved through the improvements that we had achieved, we had been able to experience a number of sessions in the computer room, as well as extra art classes, and this seemed to act as an added incentive to the pupils to continue implementing the project and keeping up the momentum.

I had now come to the end of the three-month time frame that I had allocated for my data collecting and wished to move on to the next stage of analysing my data. My pupils, however, expressed their wish to continue with the six time-saving areas we had been working on until the end of the school year. They were thus contributing to the sustainability of the research, which I regarded as an added bonus, which could have implications for the significance of the research, a concept that I will return to later in this chapter. I held one further tape-recorded discussion with my pupils, in which I asked them to consider in what ways they felt they had improved since we began the project.

New knowledge that emerges through the research process

As you engage in the task of collating your data for the purpose of determining the findings of your research, you will have a number of sources of data available to you. Your reflective journal will contain details of your reflections on your actions and any review of your action plans that may have led to a change in direction during the course of your research. You will have transcripts of any tape-recorded conversations or interviews. You may also have made video recordings or taken photographs of aspects of your research. Colleagues may have kept accounts of their observations on your research project which they could share with you at the end of your data collecting period. These various pieces of data will provide evidence to support the findings from your research and contribute to the creation of new knowledge about it. I will now outline how this process occurs in relation to the research project that I have outlined above.

My main objective was to try to eliminate the time-wasting activities in which my pupils often engaged, and which I felt was a hindrance to their learning. I sought to do this with the co-operation and collaboration of my pupils in a manner that viewed them as co-researchers. One of the first areas that we worked on was punctuality. I had noted in my research journal that five pupils, whom I shall identify by the pseudonyms Anne, Barbara, Cathy, Dorothy and Elizabeth, were consistently late for school.

A week after commencing the project, I wrote in my journal that Barbara, Cathy and Dorothy were now arriving on time for school, that Anne was still arriving late, though not as late as previously, and that it was difficult to judge whether or not Elizabeth had made any improvement as her attendance was irregular. In the final discussion with my pupils, in which I had asked whether they felt that they had improved in any way, Barbara said, 'I used to be always late but I'm coming in a bit earlier now.' (Her honesty called to mind Hopkins' (1993) view that children provide wonderfully frank and honest feedback, and this can only serve to enhance the quality of life in the classroom.) Anne, Cathy and Elizabeth attended Annabel's mathematics class and she reported that Cathy's punctuality had improved greatly, and that Anne was still occasionally late; about Elizabeth she wrote, 'Absence is a greater problem than punctuality.' Annabel's data on time-keeping, therefore, was congruent with my own data on the improvement in punctuality. The questionnaire that I asked parents to fill in contained the question, 'Has your daughter shown improvement as regards being on time for school?' Of the 19 responses I got, 18 were of the opinion that their daughter's punctuality had improved. The data outlined here provides evidence to indicate there had been an improvement in punctuality.

As you reflect on your data, you might ask yourself what you have learned from the research process. This exercise will prove useful in determining the new knowledge you have created and in formulating a theory of your practice. It will also help to move your project forward for, as Ghaye and Ghaye state, 'Creating the text is one thing; interpreting it and then using it to move thinking and practice forward is something else' (1998: 77). Your new learning may be related to your teaching practice, it may be something you have uncovered about your pupils or it may be a change in your own attitudes or opinions. The following reflective questions may help you to articulate your new learning.

Reflective activity

Ask yourself:

- What new knowledge have I gained from undertaking my research?
- What have I learned about my pupils or their learning?
- How has my new learning impacted on my self-knowledge?

I will answer these questions in relation to my research. Part of my learning from my research consisted of the realisation that regarding my pupils as co-researchers had a major impact on the research. In designating them in this way, I was treating them as equals, capable of contributing significantly to the research project. Like Hopkins (1993), I believe that it is important to involve pupils in a research project that concerns them. By consulting my pupils, I was demonstrating that I recognised them as persons with agency about educational decisions that concerned them. This is a more emancipatory approach than is often found towards research participants, particularly in the case of children, where research is often carried out 'on' rather than 'with' them. In adopting this approach, I was able to live up to my values around practising democratic principles in education and treating all pupils equally within the educational system. The knowledge that I gained in the process was that improvement in practice is more likely to occur when the terms and conditions are negotiated collaboratively with other participants rather than imposed unilaterally.

Two of the areas that we worked on related to the completion of homework and classwork. I will now discuss these issues with reference to some of the other pupils, for whom I will use pseudonyms, as with those previously mentioned.

Once we embarked on the project, I noted that in general there was an improve-ment in the amount of homework completed, and that only Barbara and Hannah still arrived in school occasionally without their copybooks. Annabel recorded that Anne and Elizabeth did not finish their mathematics homework on one occa-sion, and Cathy and Fiona did not complete their homework on another occasion. Belinda wrote that Barbara nearly always did her homework but that Hannah rarely did any work at home. On reading Belinda's comment I thought it interesting that Barbara made the following remark in one of our tape-recorded conversations: 'Since we started the project, some people are doing extra homework.' It would appear that Barbara was referring to herself in this comment. However, three out of the 19 parents who returned questionnaires to me thought that their daughters could still make a better effort at homework.

I noted that there was a greater level of improvement in completing homework, possibly because the pupils felt that if they saved time in this area, they would have an immediate reward of computer time or extra art work. The only exception to full achievement in this area was Gillian, who could not always be relied upon to get her work finished. Annabel and Belinda found that Cathy and Gillian did not always get their work done in their classes. They stated that Gillian did not seem to be able to begin a task immediately, hence her failure to complete her work in the time allotted. Many of the pupils thought they had improved in this area, as the following extracts from our final tape-recorded discussion indicate:

> Yvonne: I think I have improved by getting all my work done in school.
> Fiona: I used never [to] get my work done but now I always do.
> Vivienne: I think I have improved because I'm doing all my homework and getting my homework done.

Learning from reflection

My reflection on the improvements that occurred in the pupils' work rate and their attitude to their work helped me to realise that when pupils are encouraged to focus clearly on the task to be undertaken there are more likely to be positive outcomes. I have also learned that pupils will respond enthusiastically in attempting to achieve a goal if they know they will be rewarded for their efforts. Consequently, I devel-oped an awareness of the power of motivation as a factor in stimulating pupils towards greater achievement in the field of education. Dweck (1986) considers motivation to be a powerful force in determining how students perform in school. It is to be hoped that the stimulation that influenced the pupils to deliver optimum effort at their work in this project will sustain them into the future and have long-term consequences for their educational outcomes.

Before undertaking my research, I had noticed that my pupils did not seem to understand the concept of taking turns, as they frequently interrupted each other, and me, sometimes leading to arguments that required my intervention. Therefore I was surprised when, during our first tape-recorded discussion, they all waited their turn to speak. It created in me the expectation that, at the very least, this time-wasting activity had the potential to be eliminated. My observation proved to be correct, for I noted in my journal that in the first class discussion after starting research, only Michelle and Elizabeth spoke out of turn, and in the next discussion, there were no interruptions. Annabel said that Anne and Elizabeth continued to interrupt her when they needed individual attention, instead of raising their hand as she had asked them to do. Anne had written in her research diary, 'I did not interrupt the teacher' and I made a note in my journal to remind her that the 'no interrupting' rule applied to all teachers, not just to me! The only interruption recorded by Belinda was in the case of Gillian, who seemed to look for excuses to argue with Hannah, and there was often tension between them in the English learning support class.

As my research project progressed, I realised that the relationships that came into play in the course of the research ought to be underpinned by notions of mutual respect. I formed the opinion that all the actions that we took should be grounded in the concept of respect for all. If pupils could be encouraged to practise the value of respect for each other, then the problem of interrupting would be solved. My previous understanding of the concept of respect related mainly to the attitude of pupils towards teachers, whereas my new understanding of respect had a broader connotation. It should be all-encompassing and reciprocal, reminiscent of the capillary metaphor used by Foucault (1980b) to explain the effects of power. In other words, it should permeate all actions and interactions between pupils and teachers. The image I had of how respect should be practised was this:

pupil → pupil
teacher → pupil
pupil → teacher
teacher → teacher

I came to this new knowledge around the concept of respect through reflecting on the quality of the educational relationships that I had developed with my pupils during the course of our research project. It represented a major learning outcome for me that informed all subsequent relationships in which I engaged.

The two remaining areas of improvement that we worked on were promptness in the change-over from one subject to another and paying more attention in class. As promptness included having all books and copybooks required for a particular class, I considered Barbara and Hannah to have failed in this regard when they left copybooks at home. Annabel recorded three occasions when Anne, Cathy and Gillian did not have all the required items, but she stated that, overall, there was a big improvement in this area. Belinda noted that Barbara and Cathy occasionally forgot their homework journals, in which they wrote down their homework assignments. In our final tape-recorded conversation, Rachel remarked, 'I have improved at time saving because I always get my book out in time now.' Vivienne wrote in her research diary, 'I could improve by being quicker going to my Mathematics class' and on the following day wrote, 'I did improve, because I had all my books out and was ready to go.'

In class, I noticed that pupils were more alert and not as easily distracted as heretofore, which reduced the necessity for me to repeat instructions or to call pupils to attention. Belinda stated that Jane's attention span had improved but that Gillian tended to pay more attention to what others were doing than to her own work. In the third of our recorded discussions, Tammy remarked, 'Less people are fiddling with their hair and their pens' and in the final conversation Karen said, 'I think I have improved because I'm paying more attention.'

My learning from the final two areas of improvement stemmed from the realisation that the more organised pupils are for class in the physical sense, by having all that is required of them, the better prepared they are mentally to take in information and listen to instructions. Encouraging the trait of attentiveness in pupils can be a means towards ensuring they are alert to what is going on in their milieu. The more alert pupils are, the more likely they are to be active, rather than passive, participants, capable of making decisions in matters concerning their own educational trajectories. Active participants have the skills needed to question and critique, rather than accept unquestioningly, the knowledge that is presented to them. Ultimately, they have the potential to become creators, as opposed to recipients, of knowledge. Somekh and Zeichner claim a similar benefit through engaging in action research in the statement, 'it enabled me to give my students more empowering and engaging experiences of learning' (2009: 10).

Theories of practice

In the previous section I outlined the learning or new knowledge that emerged in the process of carrying out my research. I will now show how this knowledge can be formulated into a theory of practice. A theory of practice differs from theories found in the literature as theories in the literature are usually developed at an abstract level, whereas a theory of practice emerges from research into one's practice. Theories in the literature can prove invaluable as an aid to researchers who are formulating their theories by providing conceptual frameworks within which to locate the emerging theories of practice. The process of developing your theory of practice involves articulating the values that led you to engage in your research, reflecting on your actions to show evidence of where you are living according to your values, and examining the outcomes of your research to establish whether or not improvement has taken place. Triangulation of the research findings through the evidence provided by colleagues or critical friends can be useful in ascertaining the validity and reliability of your research.

My decision to regard my pupils as co-researchers from the beginning of my research represented the realisation of my value of equality, which I regard as particularly necessary in the field of education, if all pupils are to reach their full potential as stated as an aim of the Primary School Curriculum (Ireland, DES 1999) and in the *Review of the National Curriculum in England: Remit* (UK, DfE 2011). I would concur with Meyer's (1993) view that collaboration implies equality of relationship between researcher and participants. By considering my pupils as equal participants in the research project and accepting their insights as valid contributions to the research, I was conducting my research with, rather than on, my pupils. I was, therefore, fulfilling my commitment to democratic principles in educational provision. From these deliberations I was able to develop a theory of practice as a collaborative and co-operative space where teachers and pupils can work together to make learning a worthwhile experience for all.

An unexpected outcome of my research was the realisation of the importance of motivation in influencing pupils towards improvement. This became apparent to me when I noted during the research project that pupils were now engaging in improvement activities with little input from me. Another instance of this occurred when the pupils expressed a wish to continue with the project beyond the data collecting phase of the research. At this stage, the pupils appeared to be self-motivated. I formed a theory, therefore, that the motivation of pupils can be a key element to the success of a project, whether that motivation is extrinsic, as when I rewarded them with sessions in the computer room or art classes, or intrinsic, as when the pupils exhibited the trait of self-motivation.

I have always valued the notion of respect, but during the course of my research I came to a deeper understanding of the concept and its implications for my practice. When I discussed various aspects of the research with my pupils, I valued their opinions and appreciated their contributions. I began, therefore, to view our relationship in a new light. I now perceived it to be grounded in respect for each other as equal contributors to our research project. I began to discern a connectedness between respect and equality. If I considered someone an equal, then our relationship should be underpinned by mutual respect. Equally, if I considered it appropriate to treat others with respect, I was thereby acknowledging their right to equality of status. My learning around these issues led me to theorise my practice as promoting relationships grounded in equality of respect for all.

When I began my research I presented my pupils with research diaries in which they could note the areas for improvement and record whether or not improvement had been achieved. In this way they were introduced to the idea of reflecting on their actions, and having a voice on educational issues that directly affected them. I believed that by practising their thinking skills during the course of the research they would develop a more critical approach to their thinking in other areas. I suggest, therefore, that pupils with highly developed thinking skills are more likely to become active creators, rather than passive consumers, of knowledge and are more likely to derive long-term benefit from the educational system. The theory of practice that I developed from these insights was around the importance of encouraging independent and critical thinking skills in pupils.

Significance of the research

Undertaking an action research project can have many significant outcomes. For example, it may help you to become aware of the benefits of engaging in collaborative and co-operative initiatives with your pupils and recognising them as co-researchers capable of making considerable contributions to the project. You may learn that when relationships are based on principles of mutual respect and equality they are more likely to be productive and successful. You may also discover that pupils are capable of taking responsibility for their own learning situations. You may come to understand that having high expectations of your pupils, and empowering them to take responsibility for their actions, may result in more positive responses on their part. A significant finding for me related to the concept of motivation, in particular to the way in which the pupils, who initially were externally motivated by the promise of rewards, became self-motivated and began acting on their own initiative during the course of the research. The significance lies in the fact that self-motivated pupils have the potential to become the independent learners and critical thinkers of the future.

From the point of view of my pupils, one of the most significant outcomes was the positive attitude that was engendered in them through participating in the research. They did not at any stage contemplate the possibility of failure on their part to achieve improvement and were happy to report even the tiniest bit of improvement, as the extracts from their research diaries quoted earlier in this chapter indicate. Their social skills were further developed through their collaboration on the project, and also through overcoming the habit of interrupting each other, when they worked on that as an area for improvement. The pupils were introduced to the idea of self-reflection, when they reflected on their actions each day to determine whether there was any improvement. Through their participation in the four tape-recorded discussions that shaped our research project, they were empowered to give voice to their thoughts and ideas, and to influence the trajectory of the research. The enthusiasm that the pupils displayed for improvement in the chosen areas filtered through to other areas of school life also. For example, when they were going on a school outing, they all decided to be on their best behaviour, and when they were due to have a history test, they resolved to do some extra revision so they would do well in the test. The pupils also learned that when they managed to do their schoolwork quickly and efficiently, there was more time for the activities that they liked best, such as working with computers and art.

Your research could have significance for other educators in the wider educational community. Other teachers may have similar concerns to yours and may take inspiration from your research undertakings. Teachers wishing to improve on any area of their pupils' educational lives could benefit from learning how a rigorous and sustained self-study action research approach can achieve improvement. Teachers who have not previously worked with pupils on a research project can learn of the advantages of adopting a collaborative approach and of viewing their pupils as co-researchers. They would thus become aware of the importance of having active rather than passive learners in their classrooms, and of the significance of empowering pupils towards having a voice in educational issues that concerned them. Educators, who might be encouraged to engage in self-reflection, or to introduce that skill to their pupils, would reap the benefits of a more critical stance, which would enhance their own thinking and that of their pupils. They would thus be fulfilling the view of the teacher portrayed by Gewirtz *et al.*, who suggest that a teacher is a 'capable producer of knowledge, not reliant on experts elsewhere but as an active partner in dialogue with critical others' (2009: 571).

Of significance also to the wider educational community is the fact that the pupils, once they have reached the level of self-motivation, could contribute to the sustainability of the process of improvement. The research may have value for teachers who wish to engage in continuing professional development. It can introduce them to an action research approach, where a teacher develops a plan of action aimed at improving teaching and learning in the classroom, continuously reflects on the action to ascertain if improvement is occurring, changes the direction of the action plan if the reflection indicates this is necessary, systematically collects data, and produces findings at the end of the project. Such an approach can be a very effective way of achieving improvement for the teacher and the pupils.

Dissemination of research findings

When you finish your research project and write up your report, you may feel that matters have been brought to a conclusion and there is no need to progress beyond that point. This means that other educators do not get the opportunity to benefit from your learning through the process of carrying out your research, and the insights gained and the theories developed are denied the potential to influence a wide educational audience. However, the outcomes from a research project can be of interest to a broad spectrum of people within the educational sector, whether they are teachers working in educational institutions or policy makers with an input into the curriculum that frames teaching and learning in schools. It is important, therefore, that your findings be disseminated as widely as possible. You may choose to share the outcomes with colleagues teaching in the same school or in other local educational settings, who may be influenced to undertake similar projects, thus enabling the possibility of transformation for other teachers at the level of practice.

Another way to disseminate the findings of your research project is to present an account of the research at one of the many educational conferences that take place regularly in various countries and thus use the opportunity to share experiences and compare findings with other educators. Your research project can also be written up as an article for an educational journal, where it would be available to those working in the area of policy making, with the potential to effect theoretical transformation. In this way you have the potential to influence others at the level of theory and practice, and in the process to exert an influence on social formations (Whitehead 2004).

Chapter summary

In this chapter you have been presented with a method of developing a theory of practice from the findings of your research. You have been made aware of the importance of your values to this process, and of how the values that underpin your practice can be used to establish standards of judgement for assessing your research project. In this manner you will have come to an understanding of the inclusive nature of the relationship between theory and practice in an action research approach. You have been introduced to the idea of articulating the significance of the findings of your research at various levels. You have learned of the importance of disseminating the findings of your research so that your educative influence can have widespread effect. Finally, you will have come to the realisation that the task of trying to achieve improvement in your practice does not necessarily end with the conclusion of your research project, but can be sustained indefinitely if you continue to engage in similar research projects.

Further reading

Hitchcock, G. and Hughes, D. (1995) *Research and the Teacher: A Qualitative Introduction to School-Based Research*, 2nd edn, London: Routledge.
Gives an overview of the three main research paradigms, with particular emphasis on action research.
McNiff, J. (1988) *Action Research: Principles and Practice*, Basingstoke: Macmillan.
An excellent book for a beginner as it gives a clear account of the stages of an action research approach, which will help a practitioner to undertake a research project.
Polanyi, M. (1958) *Personal Knowledge: Towards a Post Critical Philosophy*, London: Routledge.
Outlines the importance of intuitive or tacit knowledge to the process of knowledge creation.
Whitehead, J. and McNiff, J. (2006) *Action Research Living Theory*, London: Sage Publications.
Explains how practitioners can develop their own living educational theory through carrying out research in their own lived experience.

Conclusion

We wrote this book because we wished to investigate the possibility of encouraging teachers to begin the process of enhancing their day-to-day practice through carrying out classroom-based research. When we were undertaking our postgraduate research we formed a learning community of mutual support, which was a significant factor in our ability to progress to PhD studies while continuing to teach full-time. We take the view that the collegiate approach with which we engaged can be an inspiration for you and in this book we have tried to provide you with guidelines based on our experience.

In the concluding pages of our book, we wish you well as you begin to engage with possibilities around undertaking classroom research. We have shown our personal development of critical reflection in Parts 1 and 2 so you now have an understanding that critical reflection is key to developing insight into your practice. As you move forward you might like to think about your own possible learning from the research and how it might influence your work practices into the future, as we explained in Part 4. There may be areas in which you feel that some pupils made significant progress as a result of your improved work. You could think about how you might share these discoveries with other colleagues, who might consider undertaking a similar project to yours. You could reflect on how you might influence them to begin a research process leading to improvement in their practices.

We are promoting the form of self-study action research, which we explained in this book, as a way of establishing accountability, even in teaching regimes where statutory obligations can sometimes be oppressive. Our book offers you a self-evaluatory approach to identifying yourself as a responsible professional. It gives you a way to maintain a creative, inclusive, holistic world of learning in your classroom as described in Part 3. The sharing of research generated through classroom enquiry gives teacher-researchers opportunities to contribute significant and relevant knowledge to the teaching profession.

Action research, as we explain it in this book, is real life – and real life is unpredictable, complex and fraught with uncertainty. Our theses, available on <http://www.eari.ie>, demonstrate that we each have evidence to show the enhancement in our learning. In addition they provide instances where we can show we are justified in claiming to have influenced the learning of others also. We have pointed out that the process of studying our practice did not move smoothly in a neat 'beginning–middle–end' fashion. It was messy and frequently took off into uncharted territories leading us down many warrens of confusion and perplexity. Our accounts are not 'victory narratives' (MacLure 1996) even as we celebrate the transformative aspects of our work. We each had our share of 'messy turns' (Cook 2009) while researching. We know now that the messy aspects of action research can provide rich opportunities for learning. So, using this book as a guide, you can have your professional learning from practice acknowledged. You have ideas on how to gain academic accreditation on post graduate courses for what is often called 'teacher craft knowledge' (Hagger and McIntyre 2006: 91) or the maturity of learning and teaching that comes with each successive year that you teach.

We encourage you now to take the first steps in a reflective and reflexive educational enquiry, similar to those outlined in this book, with the aim of promoting quality teaching and learning in the teaching profession. We each tried to transform our practice so as to make our classrooms and, perhaps even our schools, sites of possibility and transformation, in the hope of making the world a better place. This is not as utopian as it sounds. Kemmis (2010) agrees:

> As *researchers*, we are encouraged to make original contributions to knowledge; as *action researchers*, let us hope to do that but also to do something far more important. Let us hope to *make history* by living well, individually and collectively, and by living well *in* and *for* a world worth living in. [Italics in original.]
>
> (Kemmis 2010: 426)

We tried to become our best selves in relation to our teaching lives as we sought to improve our own understanding of why we worked as we did. We are not claiming to have all the answers – in fact we each agree that we now have lots more questions. This book contains the narrative of our honest efforts to experience our teaching lives with integrity in the hope of supporting educationalists in conducting classroom research. We feel that research based on the thinking and practice of actual classroom teachers will have a lot of credibility with other practitioners. You now have strategies to elevate your professional development to a site of empowerment and fulfilment where you can systematically analyse and improve your own practice.

The approaches outlined in this book are about how we take the view that professional development is about professional transformation rather than prescriptive technical competences methodologies. McNamara and O'Hara emphasise that 'the quality of teaching is closely bound up with the capacity of teachers to make professional research based judgements on their own practice' (2008: 21–3). We have shown you how we have set about this process. Stopping at this point, however, might not lead to sustainable improvement. We suggest that sustainable improvement will only develop through testing one's claims against identified standards of judgement (Whitehead and McNiff 2006) in a process of *continual* professional reflection and critique.

Perhaps you have now begun to think and live as an action researcher. Even after you are accreditied with your MA or your PhD, you may continue, as we have, to examine your practice and test it against your values to see if you are living them. You may have become critical and awake to the 'opening of untapped possibilities' and 'the new beginnings implicit in the educational undertaking' (Greene 2007: xvi).

We appreciate that taking action to inform understanding and improve practice can raise questions that might be difficult to answer. There may be disequilibrium as you have to shrug off hitherto comfortable but uncritically accepted norms and ways of being and thinking. If this is the case, you have indeed become critical and 'wide-awake'. You are no longer proceeding unthinkingly:

> To proceed unthinkingly is to be caught in the flux of things, to be 'caught up' in dailyness, in the sequences of tasks and routines. Of course we have to proceed that way a good deal of the time, but there should be moments when we deliberately try to draw meaning out of particular incidents and experiences. This requires a pause, a conscious effort to shake free of what Virginia Woolf called 'the nondescript cotton wool' of daily life. She associated such moments of awareness with 'moments of being': and she knew how rare they are in any given day and how necessary for the development of a sense of potency, of vital being in the world.
>
> (Greene 1984: 55)

Undertaking self-study action research and enquiring into one's practice is one way of stopping and thinking, and checking to see if what we are doing is just, fair and democratic,and for the good of others. We suggest that you cannot underestimate what might be attained by critical reflection on practice, by the identification of some areas of dissonance between the values you hold and the way you work. As we said in Chapter 2: self-study action research by you, on you, has the potential to transform your way of working, thinking and being. It also has the potential to influence others in ways you cannot yet imagine.

We invite you to have the courage to walk with us on a path of enhancing practice and developing professionally.

Bibliography

Addison Stone, C., Silliman, E.R., Ehren, B.J. and Apel, K. (2006) *Handbook of Language and Literacy: Development and Disorders*, New York: The Guilford Press.

Alexander, H. (2006) 'A View from Somewhere: Explaining the Paradigms of Educational Research', *Journal of Philosophy of Education*, 40(2), 92–120.

Alexander, R.J. (2001) *Culture and Pedagogy: International Comparisons in Primary Education*, Oxford and Boston, MA: Blackwell.

Alexander, R.J. (2008) *Essays on Pedagogy*, London: Routledge.

Altrichter, H., Feldman, A., Posh, P. and Somekh, B. (2008) *Teachers Investigate their Work: An Introduction to Action Research Across the Professions*, 2nd edn, London: Routledge.

Apple, M.W. (1996) *Cultural Politics and Education*, Buckingham: Open University Press.

Apple, M.W. (2001) *Educating the Right Way*, New York: RoutledgeFalmer.

Apple, M.W. (2004) *Ideology and Curriculum*, New York: RoutledgeFalmer.

Ashton-Warner, S. (1963) *Teacher*, London: Secker and Warburg.

Augur, J. (1986) *This Book Doesn't Make Sens, Cens, Sns, Scens, Sense*, Chichester, Sussex: Better Books.

Ayers, W. (1993) *To Teach: The Journey of a Teacher*, New York: Teachers' College Press.

Baldacchino, J. (2009) *Education Beyond Education: Self and the Imaginary in Maxine Greene's Philosophy*, New York: Peter Lang.

Ball, S.J. (2003) 'The Teacher's Soul and the Terrors of Performativity', *Journal of Education Policy*, 18(2), 215–28.

Ball, S.J. (2004) 'Education For Sale! The Commodification of Everything?', King's Annual Education Lecture 2004, University of London, 17 June 2004.

Bass, L., Anderson-Patton, V. and Allender, J. (2002) 'Self-study as a Way of Teaching and Learning: A Research Collaborative Re-analysis of Self-study Teaching Portfolios' in J. Loughran and T. Russell (eds) *Improving Teacher Education Practices Through Self-Study*, London and New York: Routledge, 55–69.

Bassey, M. (1990) *On the Nature of Research in Education*, Nottingham: Nottingham Polytechnic.

Bassey, M. (1999) *Case Study Research in Educational Settings*, Birmingham: Open University Press.

Bell, J. (1993) *Doing Your Research Project: A Guide for First-time Researchers in Education and Social Science*, 2nd edn, Buckingham and Philadelphia, PA: Open University Press.

Benhabib, S. (1987) 'The Generalized and the Concrete Other' in Eva Feder Kittay and Diana T. Myers (eds) *Women and Moral Theory*, Totowa, NJ: Rowman & Littlefield, 154–77.

Berlin, I. (1990) 'The Pursuit of the Ideal' in I. Berlin and H. Hardy (eds) *The Crooked Timber of Humanity: Chapters in the History of Ideas*, London: Pimlico.

Bohm, D. (2004) *On Dialogue*, London: Routledge.

Brown, K. (2002) *The Right to Learn*, London: RoutledgeFalmer.

Buber, M. (1958) *I and Thou*, 2nd edn, Edinburgh: T. & T. Clark.

Bullock, S.M. (2009) 'Learning to Think Like a Teacher Educator: Making the Substantive and Syntactic Structures of Teaching Explicit Through Self-study', *Teachers and Teaching: Theory and Practice*, 15(2), 291–304.

Bullough, R.V. and Pinnegar, S. (2004) 'Thinking about the Thinking about Self-study: An Analysis of Eight Chapters' in J.J. Loughran, M.L. Hamilton, V.K. LaBoskey and T. Russell (eds) *International Handbook of Self-study of Teaching and Teacher Education Practices*, vol. 1, 313–42.

Bullough, R.V. and Pinnegar, S. (2009) 'The Happiness of Teaching (as Eudaimonia): Disciplinary Knowledge and the Threat of Performativity', *Teachers and Teaching: Theory and Practice*, 15(2), 241–56.

Burbules, N. (2002) 'The Dilemma of Philosophy of Education: "Relevance" or Critique? Part Two', *Educational Theory*, Summer 2002, 52(3), 349–57.

Burbules, N. and Beck, R. (2009) 'Critical Thinking and Critical Pedagogy: Relations, Differences, and Limits', available online at <http://faculty.ed.uiuc.edu/burbules/papers/critical.html> (accessed 25 May 2008).

Bustingorry, S.O. (2008) 'Towards Teachers' Professional Autonomy Through Action Research', *Educational Action Research*, 16(3), 407–20.

Carr, W. and Kemmis, S. (1986) *Becoming Critical: Education, Knowledge and Action Research*, London: Falmer Press.

Cazden, C.B. (1988) *Classroom Discourse: The Language of Teaching and Learning*, Portsmouth, NH: Heinemann.

Chomsky, N. (2004) *Chomsky on Miseduation*, Oxford: Rowman & Littlefield.

Clandinin, D.J, (1986) *Classroom Practice: Teacher Images in Action*, London: Falmer Press.

Clandinin, D.J. and Connelly, M.F. (1995) *Teachers' Professional Knowledge Landscapes*, New York: Teachers College Press.

Clandinin, D.J., Downey, C.A. and Huber, J. (2009) 'Attending to Changing Landscapes: Shaping the Interwoven Identities of Teachers and Teacher Educators', *South Pacific Journal of Teacher Education*, 37(2), 141–54.

Cochran-Smith, M. (2003) 'Learning and Unlearning: The Education of Teacher Educators', *Teaching and Teacher Education*, 19, 5–28.

Cochran-Smith, M. and Lytle, S. (2009) *Inquiry as Stance: Practitioner Research for the Next Generation*, New York, Teachers College Press.

Cohen, L., Manion, L. and Morrison, K. (2007) *Research Methods in Education*, 6th edn, London: RoutledgeFalmer.

Cook, T. (2009) 'The Purpose of Mess in Action Research: Building Rigour Through a Messy Turn', *Educational Action Research*, 17(2), June 2009, 277–91.

Craft, A., Jeffrey B. and Liebling M (eds) (2001) *Creativity in Education*, London: Continuum.

Cremin, T., Mottram, M., Collins, F., Safford, K. (2009) 'Teachers as Readers: Building Communities of Readers', *Literacy*, 43(9), 11–19.

Croll, P. (1986) *Systematic Classroom Observation*, London: Falmer Press.

Crowell, S. (2002) 'The Spiritual Journey of a Taoist Educator' in J. Miller and Y. Nakagaw (eds) *Nurturing our Wholeness: Perspectives on Spirituality in Education*, Brandon, VT: Foundation for Educational Renewal.

Dadds, M. (1993) 'The Feeling of Thinking in Professional Self-study', *Educational Action Research*, 1(2), 287–303.

Dadds, M. (2001) 'The Politics of Pedagogy, Teachers and Teaching', *Theory and Practice*, 7(1), 43–58.

Dadds, M. and Hart, S. (2001) *Doing Practitioner Research Differently*, London: RoutledgeFalmer.

Darder, A. (1995) 'Buscando America: The Contributions of Critical Latino Educators to the Academic Development and Empowerment of Latino Students in the U.S.' in *Multicultural Education, Critical Pedagogy and the Politics of Difference*, Christine E. Sleeter and Peter L. McLaren (eds) New York: Suny Press.

Darder, A., Baltodano, M. and Torres, R.D. (eds) (2003) *The Critical Pedagogy Reader*, New York and London, Routledge.

Davies, L. (2001) 'Pupil voice and the quality of teaching and learning', paper presented at the ESRC/TLRP Consulting Pupils Network. Seminar 3: Pupil Voice and Democracy, Homerton College, University of Cambridge, 15 October.

Day, C. and Sachs, J. (2004) (eds) *International Handbook on the Continuing Professional Development of Teachers*, Maidenhead: Open University Press.

Delaney, S. (2005) 'Mathematics Professional Development for Primary Teachers: Looking Back and Looking Forward' in S. Close, T. Dooley, D. Corcoran (eds) *Proceedings of First National Conference on Research in Mathematics Education* (235–49), Dublin, Ireland: St Patrick's College.

Devine, D (2003) *Children, Power and Schooling: How Childhood is Constructed in the Primary School*, Stoke-on-Trent: Trentham Books.

Devine, D. (2004) 'School matters – listening to what children have to say' in J. Deegan, J.D. Devine and A. Lodge (2004) (eds) *Primary Voices: Equality, Diversity and Childhood in Irish Primary Schools*, Dublin: Institute of Public Administration.

DeWalt, K.M. and DeWalt, B.R. (2002) *Participant Observation*, Walnut Creek, CA: AltaMira Press.

Dewey, J. (1897) 'My Pedagogic Creed', *School Journal*, 54, January 1897, 77–80, available online at <http://dewey.pragmatism.org/creed.html> (accessed 25 May 2011).

Dewey, J. (1916, 1966) *Democracy and Education*, New York: Free Press.

Dewey, J. (1933) *How We Think: A Restatement of the Relation of Reflective Thinking to the Educative Process*, Chicago, IL: Henry Regnery.

Díaz-Andrade, A. (2009) 'Interpretive Research Aiming at Theory Building: Adopting the Case Study Design', *The Qualitative Report*, 4(1), March, 42–60, available online at <http://www.nova.edu/ssss/QR/QR14-1/diaz-andrade.pdf> (accessed on 25 May 2011).

Donaldson, M. (1978) *Children's Minds*, Glasgow: Fontana Collins.

Donham, J., Heinrich, J.A. and Bostwick, K.A. (2010) 'Mental Models of Research: Authentic Questions', *College Teaching*, 58, 8–14.

Donnelly, P. (1994) 'Thinking Time, Philosophy with Children: The Educational, Psychological and Philosophical Rationale for Doing Philosophy with Primary School Children', unpublished MEd thesis, Open University, Milton Keynes.

Dweck, C. (1986) 'Motivational Processes Affecting Learning' in A. Pollard (ed.) (1996) *Readings for Reflective Teaching in the Primary School*, London: Cassell, 119–21.

Elliott, J. (1976) *Developing Hypotheses About Classrooms from Teachers' Practical Constructs*, Grand Forks: North Dakota Study Group on Evaluation, University of North Dakota.

Elliott, J. (1991) *Action Research for Educational Change*, Buckingham: Open University Press.

Elliott, J (2004a) 'Making Evidence-based Practice Educational' in G. Thomas and R. Pring (eds) *Evidence-Based Practice in Education*, Maidenhead: Open University Press, 164–86.

Elliott, J. (2004b) 'Using Research to Improve Practice: The Notion of Evidence-based Practice' in C. Day and J. Sachs (eds) *International Handbook on the Continuing Professional Development of Teachers*, Maidenhead: Open University Press, 264–91.

Erickson, F. (1993) 'Transformation and School Success: The Politics and Culture of Educational Achievement' in E. Jacob and C. Jordan (eds) *Minority Education: Anthropological Perspectives*, Norwood, NJ: Ablex.

Feldman, S.P. (2002) *Memory as a Moral Decision: The Role of Ethics in Organizational Culture*, Piscataway, NJ: Transaction.

Fisher, R. (1990) *Teaching Children to Think*, Cheltenham: Stanley Thorne.

Fisher, R. (1995) *Teaching Children to Learn*, Cheltenham: Stanley Thorne.

Fisher, R. (1996) *Stories for Thinking*, Oxford: Nash Pollock.

Fiumara, G. (1990) trans. Charles Lambert, *The Other Side of Language: A philosophy of Listening*, London and New York: Routledge.

Flanders, N.A. (1970) *Analyzing Teaching Behaviour*, London: Addison Wesley.

Foucault, M. (1980a) 'The Eye of Power' in C. Gordon (ed) *Selected Interviews and Other Writings 1972–1977*, Brighton: Harvester Press.

Foucault, M. (1980b) *Power/Knowledge: Selected Interviews and Other Writings 1972–1977*, translated by Colin Gordon, Brighton: Harvester Press.

Foulger, T.S. (2010) 'External Conversations: An Unexpected Discovery about the Critical Friend in Action Research Inquiries', *Action Research Journal*, 2, 8 June, 135–52.

Freire, P. (1970) *Pedagogy of the Oppressed*, New York: Seabury.

Freire, P. (1972) *Pedagogy of the Oppressed*, London: Sheed & Ward.

Freire, P. (2003) 'From Pedagogy of the Oppressed' in A. Darder, M. Baltodani and R.D. Torres (eds) *The Critical Pedagogy Reader*, London: RoutledgeFalmer, 57–68.

Gardner, H. (1983) *Frames of Mind: The Theory of Multiple Intelligences*, London: Fontana Press.

Gersten, R., Fuchs, L.S., Williams, J.P. and Baker, S. (2001) 'Teaching Reading Comprehension Strategies to Students With Learning Disabilities: A Review of Research', *Review of Educational Research*, 71(2), 279–320.

Gerrish, K. and Lacey, A. (2010) *The Research Process in Nursing*, Chichester, Sussex: Wiley Blackwell.

Gewirtz, S., Shapiro, J., Maguire, M., Mahony, P. and Cribb, A (2009) 'Doing Teacher Research: A Qualitative Analysis of Purposes, Processes and Experiences', *Educational Action Research*, 17(4), 567–83.

Ghaye, A. and Ghaye, K. (1998) *Teaching and Learning through Critical Reflective Practice*, London: David Fulton.

Ghaye, T. (2011) *Teaching and Learning through Reflective Practice: A Practical Guide for Positive Action*, 2nd edn, London: Routledge.

Glenn, M. (2006) 'Working with Collaborative Projects: My Living Theory of a Holistic Educational Practice', unpublished PhD thesis, University of Limerick, available online at <http://www.eari.ie> (accessed 25 May 2011).

Glesne, C. and Peshkin, P. (1992) *Becoming Qualitative Researchers: An introduction*, New York: Longman.

Government of Ireland (2000) *National Children's Strategy: Our Children – Their Lives*, Dublin: Stationery Office.

Greene, M. (1973) *Teacher as Stranger*, New York: Wadsworth Publishing Company.

Greene, M. (1978) *Landscapes of Learning*, New York: Teachers College Press.

Greene, M. (1984) 'How Do We Think About Our Craft?', *Teachers College Record*, 86(1), 55–67.

Greene, M. (1988) *The Dialectic of Freedom*, John Dewey Lecture Series, New York: Teachers College Press.

Greene, M. (2007) *The Public School and the Private Vision: A Search for America in Education and Literature*, New York: The New Press.

Groundwater-Smith, S. and Mockler, N. (2009) *Teacher Professional Learning in an Age of Compliance: Mind the Gap*, Professional Learning and Development in Schools and Higher Education series, vol. 2, London: Springer.

Guba, E.G. and Lincoln, Y.S. (2005) 'Paradigmatic Controversies, Contradictions, and Emerging Influences' in N.K. Denzin and Y.S. Lincoln (eds) *The Sage Handbook of Qualitative Research*, 3rd edn, Thousand Oaks, CA: Sage.

Hagger, H. and McIntyre, D.(2006) *Learning Teaching from Teachers: Realising the Potential of School-based Teacher Education*, Maidenhead: Open University Press.

Hamilton, M.L. and Pinnegar, S. (1998) 'The Value and the Promise of Self-study' in M.L. Hamilton (ed.) *Reconceptualising Teaching Practice: Self-study in Teacher Education*, London: Falmer Press, 235–46.

Hammersley, M. (2004) 'Some Questions about Evidence-based Practice in Education' in G. Thomas and R. Pring (eds) *Evidence-based Practice in Education*, Maidenhead: Open University Press.

Hargreaves, A. (1994) *Changing Teachers, Changing Times: Teachers' Work and Culture in the Postmodern Age*, London: Cassell.

Hartog, M. (2004) *A Self Study Of A Higher Education Tutor: How Can I Improve My Practice?*, available online at <http://www.actionresearch.net/living/hartogphd/mhack.pdf> (accessed 25 May 2011).

Hatton, N. and Smith, D. (1995) 'Reflection in Teacher Education – Towards Definition and Implementation', *Teaching and Teacher Education*, 1191), 33–49.

Haynes, J. (2002) *Children as Philosophers: Learning Through Enquiry and Dialogue in the Primary Classroom*, London and New York: RoutledgeFalmer.

Hitchcock, G. and Hughes, D. (1995) *Research and the Teacher: A Qualitative Introduction to School-Based Research*, 2nd edn, London: Routledge.

Holley, E. (1997) 'How do I as a Teacher Researcher Contribute to the Development of a Living Educational Theory Through an Exploration of my Values in my Professional Practice?', unpublished MPhil thesis, University of Bath, available online at <http://www.actionresearch.net/living/erica.shtml> (accessed 25 May 2011).

Holt, J. (1964) *How Children Fail*, London: Penguin.

hooks, b. (2003) *Teaching Community: A Pedagogy of Hope*, New York: Routledge.

hooks, b. (2010) *Teaching Critical Thinking: Practical Wisdom*, New York: Routledge.

Hopkins, D. (1993) *A Teacher's Guide to Classroom Research*, 2nd edn, Buckingham: Open University Press.

Iaani, F.A. (1996) 'The Caring Community as a Context for Joining Youth Needs and Program Services', *Journal of Negro Education*, 65(1), 71–91.

Ireland, Department of Education and Science (1999) *Primary School Curriculum*, Dublin: Government Stationery Office.

Ireland, Department of Education and Skills (2009) *Whole School Reports*, Dublin: The Inspectorate, available online at <http://www.education.ie/insreports/school_inspection_report_listing.htm> (accessed 25 May 2011).

Jeffrey, B. and Woods, P. (1998) *Testing Teachers: The Effect of School Inspections on Primary Teachers*, London: Falmer Press.

Johnson, K.E. and Golombek, P.R. (2002) *Teacher's Narrative Enquiry as Professional Development*. Cambridge, New York and Melbourne: Cambridge University Press.

Kemmis, S. (2006) 'Participatory Action Research and the Public Sphere', *Educational Action Research*, 14(4), 459–76.

Kemmis, S. (2010) 'What is to be Done? The Place of Action Research', *Educational Action Research*, 18(4), 417–27.

Kemmis, S. and McTaggart, R. (eds) (1988) *The Action Research Planner*, 3rd edn, Geelong, Victoria: Deakin University Press.

Kerry, T. and Wilding, M. (2004) *Effective Classroom Teacher: Developing the Skills You Need in Today's Classroom*, Harlow, Essex: Pearson Longman.

Kincheloe, J.L. (2003) *Teachers as Researchers: Qualitative Inquiry as a Path to Empowerment*, 2nd edn, London and New York: Routledge.

Kincheloe, J.L. (2008) *Critical Pedagogy Primer (Peter Lang Primer)*, New York: Peter Lang.

Koshy, V. (2009) *Action Research for Improving Educational Practice*, London and Thousand Oaks CA: Sage.

Kozol, J. (2007) *Letters to a Young Teacher*, New York: Crown Publishing.

Labaree, D. (2006) *The Trouble with Ed Schools*, New Haven, CA: Yale University Press.

LaBoskey, V.K. (2004) 'The Methodology of Self-study and its Theoretical Underpinnings' in J.J. Loughran, M.L. Hamilton, V.K. LaBoskey and T. Russell (eds) *International Handbook of Self-study of Teaching and Teacher Education Practices: Part Two*, 817–70.

Ladson-Billings, G.J. (1995) 'Toward a Theory of Culturally Relevant Pedagogy', *American Education Research Journal*, 35, 465–91.

Lather, P. (2006) 'Paradigm Proliferation as a Good Thing to Think With: Teaching Research in Education as a Wild Profusion', *International Journal of Qualitative Studies in Education*, 19(1), January–February, 35–57.

Lewin, K. (1948) *Resolving Social Conflicts: Selected Papers on Group Dynamics*, edited by G.W. Lewin, New York: Harper & Row.

Lin, Qiuyun (2001) Toward a Caring-centred Multicultural Education within the Social Justice Context, available online at <http://findarticles.com/p/articles/mi_qa3673/is_1_122/ai_n28879475/> (accessed 25 May 2011).

Lipman, M. (1982) 'Philosophy for Children', *Thinking: The Journal of Philosophy for Children*, 3(4), 35–44.

Littman, C. and Stodolsky, S. (1998) 'The Professional Reading of High School Academic Teachers', *Journal of Educational Research*, 92(2), 75.

Lobel, A. (1971) *Frog and Toad are Friends.* London: HarperCollins.

Lomax, P. (2000) 'Coming to a Better Understanding of Educative Relations through Learning from Individuals' Representations of their Action Research', *Reflective Practice*, 1(1), 43–55.

Lomax, P. and Whitehead, J. (1996) 'How Do We Create Educational Responses to the Politics of Oppression?', presentation to the International Conference of the Collaborative Action Research Network, Longhirst Hall, Northumberland, 18–20 October.

Lortie, D. (1975) *Schoolteacher: A Sociological Study*, Chicago, IL: University of Chicago Press.

Loughran, J.J. (2002) 'Effective Reflective Practice: In Search of Meaning in Learning about Teaching', *Journal of Teaching Education*, 53(1), 33–43.

Loughran, J.J. (2010) *What Expert Teachers Do: Teachers' Professional Knowledge of Classroom Practice*, Sydney: Allen and Unwin, London: Routledge.

Loughran, J.J., Hamilton, M.L., LaBoskey, V.K. and Russell, T. (eds) (2004) *International Handbook of Self-study of Teaching and Teacher Education Practices*, Netherlands: Kluwer Academic Publishers.

Lynch, K. (1999) *Equality in Education*, Dublin: Gill and Macmillan.

Lyotard, J.-F. (1986) *The Postmodern Condition: A Report on Knowledge*, Manchester: Manchester University Press.

MacLure, M. (1993) 'Arguing for Yourself: Identity as an Organising Principle in Teachers' Jobs and Lives', *British Educational Research Journal*, 19(4), 311–22.

MacLure, M. (1996) 'Telling Transitions: Boundary Work in Narratives of Becoming an Action Researcher', *British Educational Research Journal*, 22(3), 273–86.

Mann, S. (2002) 'Talking Ourselves into Understanding' in K. Johnson and P. Golombek (eds), *Teacher's Narrative Enquiry as Professional Development*, Cambridge, New York and Melbourne: Cambridge University Press, 159–209.

Marcos, J.J., Sánchez, E. and Tillema, H. (2008) 'Teachers Reflecting on their Work: Articulating What is Said about What is Done', *Teachers and Teaching: Theory and Practice*, 14(2), 95–114.

Marshall, S. (1968) *An Experiment in Education*, Cambridge: Cambridge University Press.

Martin, A. and Russell, T. (2009) 'Seeing Teaching as a Discipline in the Context of Preservice Teacher Education: Insights, Confounding Issues, and Fundamental Questions', *Teachers and Teaching: Theory and Practice*, 15(2), 319–31.

McCall, C. (2009) *Transforming Thinking: Philosophical Inquiry in the Primary and Secondary Classroom*, London and New York: David Fulton.

McDonagh, C. (2007) 'My Living Theory of Learning to Teach for Social Justice: How do I Enable Primary School Children with Specific Learning Disability (Dyslexia) and Myself as Their Teacher to Realise our Learning Potentials?', PhD thesis, University of Limerick, available online at <http://www.eari.ie> (accessed 25 May 2011).

McDonagh, C. (2009) *How Do I Improve my Teaching of Children with Dyslexia: A Living Theory of Learning to Teach for Social Justice*, Saarbrücken, Germany: VDM Verlag.

McIntosh, P. (2010) *Action Research and Reflective Practice: Creative and Visual Methods to Facilitate Reflection and Learning*, London: Routledge.

McLaren, P. (2003) 'Revolutionary Pedagogy in Post-Revolutionary Times: Rethinking the Political Economy of Critical Education' in A. Darder, M. Baltodani and R.D. Torres (eds) *The Critical Pedagogy Reader*, London: RoutledgeFalmer, 151–84.

McNamara, G. and O'Hara, J. (2008) *Trusting Schools and Teachers: Developing Educational Professionalism through Self-Evaluation*, New York: Peter Lang.

McNiff, J. (1988) *Action Research: Principles and Practice*, Basingstoke: Macmillan.

McNiff, J. (2002) *Action Research for Professional Development: Concise Advice for New Action Researchers*, 3rd edn,, available online at <http://www.jeanmcniff.com/ar-booklet.asp> (accessed 25 May 2011).

McNiff, J. (2005) *Action Research for Teachers: A Practical Guide*, London: David Fulton.

McNiff, J. (2006) 'Beyond Alterity: Creating my Post-critical Living Theory of Transformational Identity', paper presented at the British Educational Research Association annual meeting, University of Warwick, 8 September 2006.

McNiff, J. (2010) *Action Research for Professional Development: Concise Advice for New and Experienced Action Researchers*, Poole, Dorset: September Books.

McNiff, J. and Whitehead, J. (2002) *Action Research: Principles and Practice*, London: RoutledgeFalmer.

McNiff, J. and Whitehead, J. (2005) *Action Research for Teachers: A Practical Guide*, London: David Fulton.

McNiff, J. and Whitehead, J. (2006) *All You Need To Know About Action Research*, London and New York: Sage.

McNiff, J. and Whitehead, J. (2009) *Doing and Writing Action Research*, London: Sage Publications.

McNiff, J. and Whitehead, J. (2010) *You and Your Action Research Project*, 3rd edn, London: RoutledgeFalmer.

McNiff, J. and Whitehead, A.J. (2011) *All You Need to Know about Action Research*, 2nd edn, London: Sage

McNiff, J., Lomax, P and Whitehead, J. (2003) *You and Your Action Research Project*, 2nd edn, London: RoutledgeFalmer.

Mellor, N. (1998) 'Notes from a Method', *Educational Action Research*, 6(3), 453–70.

Mellor, N. (2001) 'Messy Method: The Unfolding Story', *Educational Action Research*, 9(3), 465–84.

Meyer, J.E. (1993) 'New Paradigm Research in Practice: The Trials and Tribulations of Action Research' in *Journal of Advanced Nursing*, 18, 1066–72.

Miller, J. (1996) *The Holistic Curriculum*, Toronto: Ontario Institute for Studies in Education Press.

Miller, J. (2007) *The Holistic Curriculum*, 2nd edn, Toronto: University of Toronto Press.

Moon, J. (2004) *A Handbook of Reflective and Experiential Learning: Theory and Practice*, London and New York: RoutledgeFalmer.

Mosley, J. (1998) *Quality Circle Time in the Primary Classroom*, London: LDA Learning.

Murphy, B. (2004) 'Social Interaction and Language Use in Irish Infant Classrooms in the Context of the Revised Irish Primary School Curriculum (1999)', *Literacy*, November, 149–55.

Murris, K. (2000) 'Can Children do Philosophy?', *Journal of Philosophy of Education*, Summer, 261–80.

Nash-Wortham, M. and Hunt, J. (1993) *Take Time*, Stourbridge, West Midlands: Robinswood Press.

National Council for Curriculum Assessment (2007) *Assessment in the Primary School Curriculum – Guidelines for Schools*, Ireland: NCCA.

Newton, I. (1675) Letter to Robert Hooke, 5 February 1675, available online at <http://www.quotationspage.com/quotes/Isaac_Newton/> (accessed 25 May 2011).

Noddings, N (1984) *Caring: A Feminine Approach to Ethics and Moral Education*, Berkeley and Los Angeles: University of California Press.

Noddings, N. (1992) *The Challenge to Care in Schools: An Alternative Approach to Education*, New York: Teachers College Press.

Noddings, N. (2005) *The Challenge to Care in Schools: an Alternative Approach to Education*, 2nd edn, New York: Teachers College Press.

Noffke, S. and Somekh, B. (2009) *The SAGE Handbook of Educational Action Research*, London: Sage.

O'Donoghue, T. and Punch, K. (2003) *Qualitative Educational Research in Action: Doing and Reflecting*, London: Routledge.

O'Hanlon, C. (2002) 'Reflection and Action in Research: Is There a Moral Responsibility to Act?' in C. Day, J. Elliott, B. Somekh and R. Winter (eds) *Theory and Practice in Action Research*, Oxford: Symposium Books, 111–20.

P4C (n.d.) <http://p4c.com/> (accessed 28 January 2011).

Palmer, P.J. (1993) *To Know as We are Known: Education as a Spiritual Journey*, New York: HarperCollins.

Palmer, P.J. (1998) *The Courage to Teach: Exploring the Inner Landscape of a Teacher's Landscape*, San Francisco: Jossey-Bass.

Palmer, P.J. (2007) *The Courage to Teach: Exploring the Inner Landscape of a Teacher's Life*, 10th edn, San Francisco: Jossey-Bass.

Parsons, L.T. (2004) 'Ella Evolving: Cinderella Stories and the Construction of Gender-Appropriate Behavior', *Children's Literature in Education*, 35(2), 135–54.

Pithouse, K., Mitchell, C. and Weber, S. (2009) 'Self-study in Teaching and Teacher Development: A Call to Action', *Educational Action Research*, 17(1), 43–62.

Polanyi, M. (1958) *Personal Knowledge: Towards a Post Critical Philosophy*, London: Routledge.

Polanyi, M. (1967) *The Tacit Dimension*, New York: Anchor Books.

Pollard, A. (ed.) (2008) *Readings for Reflective Teaching*, London and New York: Continuum.

Postholm, M.B. (2009) 'Research and Development Work: Developing Teachers as Researchers or Just Teachers?', *Educational Action Research*, 17(4), 551–65.

Quinn, V. (1997) *Critical Thinking in Young Minds*, London: David Fulton.

Raz, J. (2001) *Value, Respect and Attachment*, Cambridge: Cambridge University Press.

Rice, S. and Burbules, N. (2010) 'Listening: A Virtue Account', *Teachers College Record*, 112(11), 2728–42.

Riel, M., (1999) *The Internet: A Land to Settle Rather Than an Ocean to Surf*, available online at <http://www.globalschoolnet.org/gsh/teach/articles/netasplace.html> (accessed 25 May 2011).

Robson, C. (1993) *Real World Research: a Resource for Social Scientists and Practitioner-Researchers*, Oxford: Blackwell.

Roche, M. (2000) 'How Do I Help My Pupils to Philosophise?', unpublished MEd thesis, UWE Bristol, available online at <http://www.eari.ie> (accessed 25 May 2011).

Roche, M. (2007) 'Towards a Living Theory of Caring Pedagogy: Interrogating My Practice to Nurture a Critical, Emancipatory and Just Community of Enquiry', unpublished PhD thesis, University of Limerick, available online at <http://www.eari.ie> (accessed 25 May 2011).

Roche, M. (2011) 'Creating a Dialogical and Critical Classroom: Reflection and Action to Improve Practice', *Educational Action Research*, 19(3), 327–43

Ruddock, J. and Fielding, M. (2006) 'Student Voice and the Peril of Popularity', *Educational Review*, 58(2), 219–31.

Ruddock, J. and McIntyre, D. (2007) *Improving Learning Through Consulting Pupils*, London: Routledge.

Rudland, N. and Kemp, C. (2004) 'The Professional Reading Habits of Teachers: Implications for Student Learning', *Australasian Journal of Special Education*, 28(1), 2004, 4–17.

Russell, T. (2002) 'Can Self-study Improve Teacher Education?' in J. Loughran and T. Russell (eds) *Improving Teacher Education Practices Through Self-study*, London: RoutledgeFalmer.

Sachs, J. (2003) *The Activist Teaching Profession*, Buckingham: Open University Press.

Said, E. (1994) *Beginnings: Intention and Method*, London: Granta.

Samaras, A.P. and Freese, A.R. (2006) *Self-study of Teaching Practices Primer*, New York: Peter Lang.

Scherff, L. and Kaplan, J. (2006) 'Reality Check: A Teacher Educator Returns Home', *Studying Teacher Education*, 2, 155–67.

Schmertzing, R. (2007) 'Expert Researchers and School Practitioners: An Historical Perspective on the Marginalization of Practitioner Research and the Silencing of Practitioner Voices', *Journal of Education*, 188(1), 1–24.

Schön, D. (1983) *The Reflective Practitioner: How Professionals Think in Action*, New York: Basic Books.

Schön, D. (1995) 'Knowing in Action: The New Scholarship Requires a New Epistemology', *Change*, November–December, 27–34.

Shaywitz, S. and Shaywitz, B. (2005) 'Dyslexia (Specific Reading Disability)', *Biological Psychiatry*, 57(11), 1301–9.

Shermis, S.S. (1992) *Critical Thinking: Helping Students Learn Reflectively*, Bloomington, IN: ERIC Clearinghouse on Reading and Communication Skills.

Shulman, L.S. (2002) 'Forgive and Remember: The Challenges and Opportunities of Learning from Experience', *Launching the Next Generation of New Teachers*, Symposium Proceedings, January 2002, New Teacher Center at the University of California, Santa Cruz.

Skamp, K. and Mueller, A. (2001) 'Student Teachers' Conceptions about Effective Primary Science Teaching: A Longitudinal Study', *International Journal of Science Education*, 23(4), 331–51.

Skinner, B. (1957) *Verbal Behaviour*, New York: Appleton-Century-Crofts.

Skinner, B.F. (1954) 'The Science of Learning and the Art of Teaching', *Harvard Educational Review*, 24, 86–97.

Somekh, B. (2010) 'The Collaborative Action Research Network: 30 Years of Agency in Developing Educational Action Research', *Educational Action Research*, 18(1), 103–21.

Somekh, B. and Zeichner, K. (2009) 'Action Research for Educational Reform: Remodelling Action Research Theories and Practices in Local Contexts', *Educational Action Research*, 17(1), 5–21.

Stenhouse, L. (1975) *An Introduction to Curriculum Research and Development*, London: Heinemann.

Stenhouse, L. (1983) 'Towards a Vernacular of Humanisim' in L. Stenhouse, *Authority, Education and Emancipation: A Collection of Papers*, London: Heinemann.

Stoll, L., Fink, D. and Earl, L. (2003) *It's About Learning (and It's About Time)*, London: RoutledgeFalmer.

Sullivan, B. (2000) 'How Can I Help My Pupils to Make More Effective Use of Their Time in School?, unpublished MA dissertation, University of the West of England, Bristol.

Sullivan, B. (2006) 'A Living Theory of a Practice of Social Justice: Realising the Right of Traveller Children to Educational Equality', unpublished PhD thesis, University of Limerick, available online at <http://www.eari.ie> (accessed 25 May 2011).

Taylor C. and White S. (2000) *Practising Reflexivity in Health and Welfare; Making Knowledge*, Buckingham: Open University Press.

Teaching Council of Ireland (2009) *The Professional Body for Teaching*, available online at <http://www.teaching council.ie/TCPublications/TC Info book ENG> (accessed June 2011).

Trelease, J. (2007) *How Non-reading Students are Related to their Non-reading Parents and Teachers: Excerpts from The Read-Aloud Handbook*, available online at <http://www.trelease-on-reading.com/whatsnu_morrie.html> (accessed 25 May 2011).

Trickey, S. and Topping K.J. (2004) 'Philosophy for Children: A Systematic Review', *Research Papers in Education*, 19(3), 365–80.

Trousdale, A.M. and McMillan, S. (2003) '"Cinderella Was a Wuss": A Young Girl's Responses to Feminist and Patriarchal Folktales', *Children's Literature in Education*, 34(1), 1–29.

UK, Department for Education (2011) *Review of the National Curriculum in England: Remit*, available online at <http://www.education.gov.uk/schools/teachingandlearning/curriculumb0073043/remit-for-review-of-the-national-curriculum-in-england> (accessed 25 May 2011).

Vygotsky, L.S. (1962) *Thought and Language*, Cambridge, MA: MIT Press.

Vygotsky, L.S. (1978) *Mind in Society*, Cambridge, MA: Harvard University Press.

Whitehead, J. (1989) 'Creating a Living Educational Theory from Questions of the Kind, "How Do I Improve My Practice?"', *Cambridge Journal of Education*, 19(1), 41–52, available online at <http://www.actionresearch.net/writings/livtheory.html> (accessed 25 May 2011).

Whitehead, J. (1993) *The Growth of Educational Knowledge: Creating Your Own Living Educational Theories*, Bournemouth: Hyde.

Whitehead, J. (2000) 'How Do I Improve My Practice? Creating and Legitimating an Epistemology of Practice', *Reflective Practice*, 1(1), 91–104.

Whitehead, J. (2003) 'What is Educational in What I Do for Myself, for Others and for the Education of Social Formations? A Contribution to a Conversation on Theory in Action Research', paper presented at *Critical Debates in Action Research*, University of Limerick, 5–7 June, 2003.

Whitehead, J. (2004) 'What Counts as Evidence in the Self-studies of Teacher Education Practices?' in J.J. Loughran, M.L. Hamilton, V.K. LaBoskey and T. Russell (eds) *International Handbook of Self-Study of Teaching and Teacher Education Practices*, available online at <http://www.actionresearch.net/writings/evid.htm> (accessed 25 May 2011).

Whitehead, J. (2005) 'Creating Educational Theories from Educational Enquiries of the Kind, "How Do I Improve My Educational Influence?" A Response to Gorard and Nash', paper submitted to *The Journal of Educational Enquiry*, 14 March.

Whitehead, J. (2007) 'The Significance of "I" in Living Educational Theories' (draft), available online at <http://www.actionresearch.net/writings/jack/jwchptroutledge150507.htm> (accessed 25 May 2011).

Whitehead, J. (2011) 'Action Research: What is a Living Educational Theory Approach to Action Research and a Human Existence?', available online at <http://www. actionresearch.net/writings/livtheory.html> (accessed June 2011).

Whitehead, J. and McNiff, J. (2006) *Action Research Living Theory*, London: Sage Publications.

Wierenga, N. (2011) 'Teachers' Educational Design as a Process of Reflection-in-Action: The Lessons We Can Learn From Donald Schön's The Reflective Practitioner When Studying the Professional Practice of Teachers as Educational Designers', *Curriculum Inquiry*, 41(1), 167–74.

Wilcox, S., Watson, J. and Patterson, M. (2004) 'Self-study in Professional Practice' in J.J. Loughran, M.L. Hamilton, V.K. La Boskey and T. Russell (eds) *International Handbook of Self-study of Teaching and Teacher Education Practices*, vol. 1, 273–312.

Wilkins, C. and Wood, P. (2009) 'Initial Teacher Education in the Panopticon', *Journal of Education for Teaching*, 35(3), 283–97.

Winter, R. (2002) 'Truth or Fiction: Problems of Validity and Authenticity in Narratives of Action Research', *Educational Action Research*, 10(1), 143–54.

Woodward, H. (1998) 'Reflective Journals and Portfolios: Learning through Assessment', *Assessment and Evaluation in Higher Education*, 23(4).

Wragg, T. (1983) 'Lawrence Stenhouse: A Memorable Man', *British Educational Research Journal*, 9(1), 3–5.

Yoshida, A. (2002) 'Martin Buber, Education as Holistic Encounter and Dialogue' in J. Miller and Y. Nakagawa (eds) *Nurturing our Wholeness: Perspectives on Spirituality in Education*, Brandon, VT: Foundation for Educational Renewal.

Young, I.M. (1990) *Justice and the Politics of Difference*, Princeton; Princeton University Press.

Young, I.M. (2000) *Inclusion and Democracy*, New York: Oxford University Press.

Zeichner, K. (2007) 'Accumulating Knowledge Across Self-studies in Teacher Education', *Journal of Teacher Education*, 58, 36–46.

Zeichner, K.M. and Liston, D.P. (1996) *Reflective Teaching: An Introduction*, Mahwah, NJ: Lawrence Erlbaum.

Index